You and the Law Series

LAW AND THE COURTS

A Handbook About United States Law and Court Procedures

WITH A GLOSSARY OF LEGAL TERMS

American Bar Association
Public Education Division

Points of view or opinions in this document are those of the author and do not necessarily represent the official position or policies of the American Bar Association or the Standing Committee on Public Education.

Library of Congress Number: 87–073126
ISBN Number: 0-89707-331-2

Produced by the ABA Press

Contents

Introduction

For most people, law and the courts are veiled in mystery. Even though the law is made by legislators elected by the public and interpreted by judges chosen directly or indirectly by the public, and even though great strides have been made in making the law and its special language more understandable to people, the general public is still often confused about law and the courts.

This booklet attempts to unravel some of these mysteries. It provides an introduction to our legal system, discusses briefly the roles of key actors in the system, and outlines and explains the steps involved in most civil and criminal cases. While it does not include all kinds of lawsuits, it does attempt to explain the procedures common to most of them.

The booklet also discusses some of the special courts in the American system, provides a chart on courts in the federal system and in a representative state, and explores various methods of alternative dispute resolution. A glossary of frequently used legal terms is included as a ready reference.

The focus of "Law and the Courts" is on helping readers understand the system as a whole. It is intended for the general public, journalists covering the courts, court observers, and anyone else who wants to become more familiar with our legal system and the role of the courts.

Practical problems of everyday law are not examined in this booklet. Other books in the "You and the Law" series cover those topics. For example, booklets in the series focus on law and marriage, landlords and tenants, consumer credit and bankruptcy, your rights over age 50, and law in the workplace. In addition, another booklet in the series, "The American

Lawyer: When and How to Use One," is designed for people who are deciding if they need a lawyer and, if so, how best to select one. It shows how lawyers are trained, the ethical responsibilities of lawyers, criteria to use in choosing a lawyer, and such alternatives to using a lawyer as small claims courts. Information on how to order these booklets can be found on the inside front and back covers of this booklet.

Acknowledgment

This revised and expanded edition of "Law and the Courts," first published in 1980, is the work of many people. The American Bar Association's Standing Committee on Public Education has overall responsibility for the booklet, which is part of its "You and the Law" series. A member of the committee, C. Thomas Ross, oversaw the project. Charles White, publications director of the ABA's Public Education Division, served as its editor. Geoff Belzer, a student intern from the Medill School of Journalism at Northwestern University, assisted the project in its early stages, reviewing the existing edition, suggesting revisions, and writing first drafts of a number of the revised chapters.

Another ABA entity—the National Conference of Lawyers and Representatives of the Media—undertook a great deal of the revision of the original text. Of particular help was conference member Ray Reynolds, a legal journalist who helped redraft the section on court procedure and the glossary. Mark Gerchick, the liaison to the Conference from the Young Lawyers Section, contributed a draft of the revised chapter on fair trial/free press, and J. Laurent Scharff, a member of the Conference, contributed several revisions to that chapter. The entire committee reviewed large portions of the draft manuscript and made many useful suggestions. In addition, the Young Lawyers Division Law and Media Committee reviewed and field tested the draft manuscript.

The draft manuscript was further reviewed by a number of ABA staff members. Providing particular assistance at the staff level were Norman Gross, Director of the Public Education Division, and a committee that reviewed several drafts of the manuscript, composed of Nancy Slonim of the Communications Department; Miriam Krasno of the *Judges' Journal*; and Wantland Sandel and Doug Somerlot of the Judicial Services Division.

Other ABA staff members contributed to individual sections of the booklet. Terry Brooks of the Legal Services Division helped write the section on disciplining judges, and Fred Melcher of the *Judges' Journal* answered a number of specific questions about the courts. Debbie Weixl of the Communications Department was a source of information on a number of free press/fair trial issues. Tom Smith of the Criminal Justice Division contributed a thorough review of the criminal procedure section of the booklet. Judith White McBride of the Evaluation of Judicial Performance project, Larry E. Ray of the Standing Committee on Dispute Resolution, and Elaine Reich of the Center for Professional Responsibility contributed paragraphs on their areas of interest.

A number of specialists on the courts provided assistance. Leonard E. Klein of the Federal Judicial Center contributed a great deal of useful information. Christine Rose of the Criminal Justice Information Center provided data on a number of points. Robert Roper, Dixie Knoebel, and Marilyn Roberts of the National Center for State Courts answered a number of specific questions, and Tom Munsterman of the National Center for Jury Studies was most helpful on several issues relating to juries. Kate Sampson of the American Judicature Society contributed much useful information on merit selection of judges.

Jack Doppelt and his students in the legal reporting class at the Medill School of Journalism of Northwestern University reviewed the manuscript and suggested several revisions. Various drafts were also reviewed by persons who have an interest in the courts but are neither lawyers nor journalists. We particularly thank Sue Melcher for her thoughtful comments and questions.

The manuscript was also reviewed by a number of lawyers, judges, and court administrators, who suggested many stylistic and substantive improvements. We thank Shirley S. Abrahamson, Luther Avery, Michael E. Barber, Sherwin Birnkrant, John Corderman, Michael Franck, Janice Gradwohl, John Graecen, E. D. Hieronymus, Thomas S. Hodson, Gregory P. Joseph, Warren Levy, Francis J. O'Byrne, Sherman S. Poland, Ed Schoenbaum, and Robert Yegge.

The scope of the original "Law and the Courts" has been broadened in this edition by material on the role of law, the adversary system, the function of courts and special tribunals, and the responsibilities of lawyers, judges, and other important actors in the system. Many of these added sections, as well as portions of the glossary, are adapted from Lyle Denniston's *The Reporter and the Law* (New York: Hastings House, 1980), a comprehensive account of considerable value to anyone who wants to pursue the subject in more detail. We thank Mr. Denniston for permission to adapt his work.

Additional material on the federal courts and the chart outlining the federal system were adapted from "The United States Courts: Their Jurisdiction and Work," a publication of the Administrative Office of the U.S. Courts. We thank the Office for permission to adapt portions of the booklet.

The chart on the court system of Florida is adapted from *State Court Caseload Statistics: Annual Report 1984*, a publication of the National Center for State Courts. We thank the Center for permitting us to use this chart.

Law and the Courts

What is the function of law? Most people think of the law as prohibitive or punitive—the police officer arresting a suspect or a judge imposing sentence on a defendant. That can be true of criminal law, at least up to a point, but it overlooks the role of law in regulating disputes and providing for a rational and civilized way of ordering society. In this sense, the law is an enabler, something that *permits* us to enjoy rights within the framework of an ordered society.

In many ways law is the cornerstone of our culture. The rule of law provides society with the rules by which all of us live. Citizens can know the law and live their lives accordingly. Conversely, citizens have the right to rely on the law and be confident of the protection provided by the courts.

The courts have the duty of applying the law to specific controversies brought before them. Courts resolve disputes between people, legal entities and units of government. They are often called upon to uphold limitations on the government, to protect against possible abuses of the law-making and law-enforcing branches of government, to protect minorities of all types from the majority, and to protect the rights of people who can't protect themselves.

The rule of law also incorporates notions of equal treatment and fair play. Under the rule of law, no person is above the law—and no person is below it. The courts—and the protections of the law—are open to everybody.

A recent survey of judges and court administrators revealed agreement about the following basic purposes of courts:

1. To do justice in individual cases.
2. To adhere to standards of impartiality and fair procedure, so that the courts are credible to the public and their procedures predictable to lawyers.
3. To provide a forum for the resolution of disputes and a non-violent form of dispute resolution; there must be finality of results and prompt resolution to allow people to get on with their lives.
4. To protect individuals from arbitrary use of government power. The U.S. Constitution creates a government of *limited* power. For example, the government must allow most defendants to go free on bail while they await trial. It must not conduct secret trials or conduct unreasonable searches and seizures. It is the courts which enforce these protections of the individual. Through the courts, governmental powers are kept within legal limits.
5. To make a formal record of legal status. Many non-trial or non-contested court proceedings exist to develop a record of the change of legal status, *e.g.*, estates of those who have died; marriage; non-contested divorce; adoption; garnishment; attachment; transfer of real property. Many court employees, such as court reporters and clerks of courts, perform this record-keeping function. Courts spend a substantial portion of their budgets on record keeping.
6. To deter criminal behavior by people other than the defendant; to rehabilitate persons convicted of crime; to separate convicted persons from society.
7. To inform the public, through court decisions, about what behavior is lawful and what behavior is unlawful.

Lloyd N. Cutler, a former counsel to President Carter, writes of the judiciary:

> It has the greatest respect among the propertied and the underprivileged classes. One, because of all the institutions it has worked the best and, two, because . . . it has upheld the rights of minorities. The judiciary is now looked on as the defender of everyone's rights.

THE ADVERSARY SYSTEM

Examples of courts providing a means of impartial decision-making are found throughout our system. For example, our legal system is based on the adversary process. The adversary process is grounded on the idea that the best way to get to the truth is to allow all of the competing parties to present their views to an impartial third party as adversaries, or opponents, under rules that permit the evidence to be presented fairly and in an orderly fashion. A trial under the adversary process is designed to (1) determine the facts, (2) determine governing law, (3) apply law to the facts and (4) resolve disputes by awarding (or denying) judgment. In the end, it is the impartial third party—the judge or jury—who decides the case based on the evidence presented.

To the general public, the adversary system may look like game playing. Concepts such as "burden of proof" and standards of proof such as "beyond a reasonable doubt" or "more probable than not" may mean very little to most people. However, these distinctions mean everything to an accused person who must be "more probably than not" guilty of an offense to be indicted (charged with a crime), but must be proved guilty "beyond a reasonable doubt" to be convicted. This distinction is an example of the law's establishing a format which permits decisions to be made rationally, under uniform standards.

Often the complex nature of the legal process is thought of as a mass of "technicalities," or "legal red tape." Yet the so-called technicalities safeguard the rights of every citizen. As this booklet notes, they ensure equal protection of the law and due process of law, which are the essence of our system of justice.

CIVIL CASES AND CRIMINAL CASES

It is important to remember, at the outset, that law deals with two kinds of cases. Civil cases, for the most part, involve the resolution of private conflicts between people or institutions; criminal cases involve the enforcement of public or official codes of behavior that society deems necessary for the protection of its citizens or of itself.

Domestic relations issues—divorce, child support, custody, and the like—are the biggest single subject of civil cases. Automobile accidents probably account for more tort actions—a very common type of civil case—than any other cause. An auto accident could give rise to a civil case if one driver sued the other, if both drivers sued each other, or if a passenger in one of the cars sued either driver.

If an accident involves allegations of illegal behavior—drunken driving, hit and run driving—it may also give rise to a criminal case. In criminal cases, the state brings charges against the person who allegedly committed the crime. In civil cases, the persons themselves bring suit.

Most disputes are not resolved through the trial process. Most legal controversies never result in lawsuits. Much of the time and energy of the legal profession is and must be spent in avoiding contests in court. That is as true in criminal cases as it is in civil cases. If that effort did not usually succeed, the courts could not possibly manage the workload they would have.

STATE COURTS AND FEDERAL COURTS

One of the most confusing aspects of our courts is that we have not one but two distinct court systems: state courts *and* federal courts.

The vast majority of cases are tried in the state courts. In 1984, for example, the most recent year for which complete statistics are available, approximately 3,275,000 civil cases were filed. Of this total, just under 3 million (92 percent) were filed in state courts, and 275,000 (8 percent) in federal courts.

State courts are established in each state under the authority of the state government. Each state is free to determine its own particular kind of court structure, under its own constitution and laws, as long as the courts operate within the limits of the U.S. Constitution. No two states have exactly the same system. State courts decide almost every type of case. They are located in many towns and almost all counties and are the courts with which most citizens have contact. The great bulk of legal business concerning divorce and the probate of estates and all other matters except those assigned to the United States courts is handled by the state courts. The chart on page 16 shows the various state courts that are available to the citizens of Florida. While no state court system can be said to be "typical," the Florida system is broadly representative of the general structure of state courts in this country.

There are far fewer federal courts, and most of them are located in the larger cities. The chart on page 17 shows the general structure of the federal courts. A case may be filed in federal court only if there is a specific federal statute or a provision in the United States Constitution granting the federal courts jurisdiction to hear the case. While there are instances of overlapping jurisdiction, cases cannot generally be tried in both systems. Most must be tried in one or the other.

The state courts differ from each other and from the federal courts in many aspects of their procedure. For that reason, generalizations about court procedure are rarely applicable across the board. Thus the procedural steps outlined in this publication (see especially pages to come) may not apply to some courts. For an in-depth look at the courts of your state, you may want to contact your state bar association, your state court administrator, or your state supreme court.

THE STRUCTURE OF COURTS

Basically, the courts of this country are divided into three layers:

- "limited" or "general jurisdiction" courts, where cases start;
- "intermediate" (appellate) courts, where appeals are first heard; and
- "supreme" courts which have final judicial authority.

This division is generally true of both state courts and federal courts.

The court systems in this country are thus organized as hierarchies. Higher courts have the power to review the work of lower courts.

However, that is a power brought to bear on a small number of cases. In fact, most cases don't even make it to trial. For example, it is estimated that 90 percent of all criminal cases are disposed of prior to trial: 60 percent are ended by a guilty plea, 30 percent are dismissed, and only the remaining 10 percent go to trial. The proportion of civil cases settled prior to trial is at least that high. And of the civil cases that do go to trial, the vast majority are decided at the trial court level and are not appealed. (Appeals are more common in criminal cases that result in conviction.)

Thus appellate courts, and in particular supreme courts, deal with a very small percentage of the total number of cases filed. For example, out of the millions of cases that are handled annually by American courts, only about 150 a year are given full-scale review by the Supreme Court of the United States.

Trial Courts. Trial courts are the courts most familiar to the general public, since they are the setting of the vast majority of courtroom dramas. It is in trial courts that evidence is taken, witnesses examined and cross-examined, and exhibits introduced. It is in trial courts that a determination of the facts is made, and judges and juries make their decision. It is in trial courts that a defendant is found "guilty" or "not guilty" in criminal cases and liability is decided in civil cases.

Trial Courts: State. In every state there are trial courts of one kind or another. Some of them exist at the city or town level, others at a county, circuit, or regional level.

Most states have some trial courts with limited jurisdiction. (A small number of states—including Massachusetts, Idaho, Illinois, Iowa, and South Dakota—have unified court systems in which there are only trial courts of general jurisdiction.) Courts of limited jurisdiction are quite important because they handle as much as 90 percent of the case load in the states in which they exist. They process minor criminal cases, such as misdemeanors, which are less serious crimes for which the penalties involve fines or jail terms of no more than one year of imprisonment. (Some states, such as North Carolina, have two-year maximums for misdemeanors.) In most jurisdictions, these courts also have authority to conduct pre-trial hearings in more serious criminal cases, including preliminary hearings at which bail is set and defendants bound over for trial. These courts also handle civil cases involving money claims up to a certain dollar amount, in some states as low as $500 and in some as much as $10,000 or more.

The names of these courts vary widely. In some states they get their names from the official title of the presiding judge: "magistrate courts" and "justice of the peace courts," for example. Some, like "traffic courts," are named because of the nature of their jurisdiction. Some have geographic names: "district courts," "municipal courts," or "county courts."

FLORIDA COURT SYSTEM

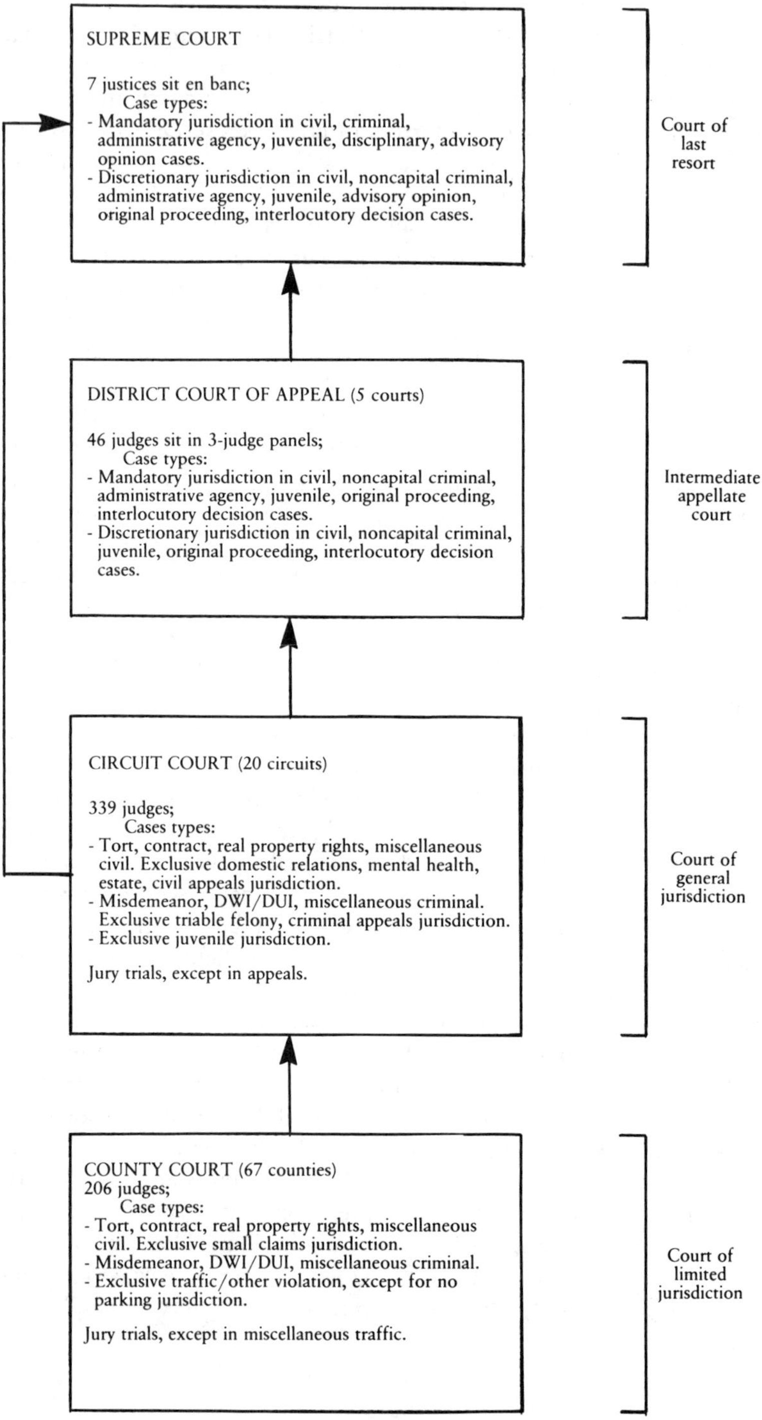

THE UNITED STATES COURT SYSTEM

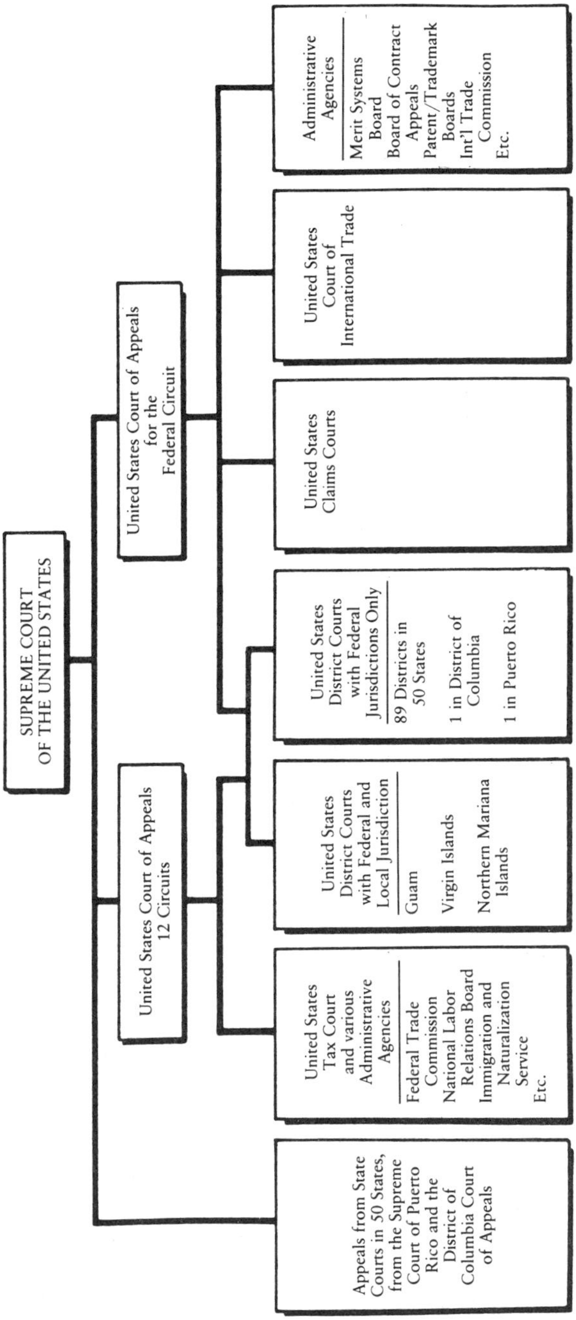

Some of these courts may use simplified, often quite informal procedures, and hearings may be quite brief. In a traffic court, for example, the entire case may be over in a few minutes, with the police officer reading a charge in formal language, a judge asking the accused for a plea and, if the plea is "guilty," then passing sentence immediately.

In many of these courts, however, procedures are formal and jury trials are used in both civil and criminal cases.

The next group of courts goes by a variety of names: "district," "superior," or "circuit" courts, or "courts of common pleas." Customarily, these tribunals have "general" jurisdiction, meaning—in most states—that they may try either civil or criminal cases without upper limits on the imposition of penalties or the amount of money involved. They generally try only the more serious criminal cases or the civil cases above a certain dollar amount. Procedures in these courts usually are quite formal and technical, and they customarily will keep verbatim records.

These courts often try cases with juries (sometimes with as few as six members in civil cases, but almost always with twelve in criminal cases). In many jurisidictions, jury trials in criminal cases are automatic unless waived by the defendant. The defendant in a criminal case or the parties in a civil case can choose not to have a trial by jury, but to be tried by a judge.

In some states, special trial courts exist to handle designated kinds of cases, such as divorce cases, cases involving last wills and other "estate" law matters, child adoption or custody cases and juvenile crime cases. (See pp. 31-34 for more on these specialized courts.)

Trial Courts: Federal. Trials in federal courts are generally held in U.S. district courts. That is the only name they have, wherever they sit, and they all are governed by the U.S. Constitution and specific federal laws as to their jurisdiction and federal rules for their basic procedures.

There are 94 federal judicial districts in the country. These federal courts have jurisdiction for their area, either an entire state or part of a state. None has jurisdiction in more than one state.

Each state contains at least one federal district. About half of the states contain only one federal district, but many have two or three districts, and California, Texas, and New York have four districts each. Each district has from one to twenty-seven judges, depending on the volume of cases that must be decided. In all, there are 575 district judgeships authorized by law (1986 figure).

No district court may handle a case unless there is federal jurisdiction—that is, express authority for the federal courts to decide a case. Not all cases in federal court involve federal law, however. If the parties in a case involving state law come from different states (diversity of citizenship), and their controversy is for $10,000 or more, one or the other of them may demand that the case be tried in U.S. district court, according to the law of the state whose law governs the dispute. The theory is that out-of-state parties have a better chance for a fair trial in a federal court than in a court of a state where their opponents are residents but they are not.

A federal statute gives federal courts jurisdiction over some state civil rights cases, which may be transferred ("removed" is the formal legal term) to a U.S. district court for trial.

The federal district courts receive more civil than criminal matters, because there are relatively few crimes under federal law. For example, in the fiscal year which ended June 30, 1985, the United States district courts received seven times more civil cases than criminal cases (273,000 civil cases and only 39,000 criminal cases). However, because the Speedy Trial Act, which relates to criminal cases, requires trial in a very short time after indictment, the federal courts may spend considerably more then one-seventh of their time on criminal matters.

In addition to the district courts, there are a few specialized trial courts in the federal system:

- Bankruptcy proceedings filed in the district courts may be referred to federal bankruptcy judges for hearing and decision. There are 232 such judges, who in a recent year received 365,000 bankruptcy petitions.
- Federal magistrates handle smaller civil and criminal matters.
- The United States Court of International Trade primarily handles cases involving international trade and customs duties. This court consists of nine judges.
- The United States Claims Court consists of 16 judges. It hears cases in which an individual citizen or corporation sues the United States government. It also has jurisdiction over other specialized areas.
- The United States Tax Court decides controversies between taxpayers and the Internal Revenue Service. It is comprised of 19 judges.

In addition, there are also military "courts-martial." These military courts are administered by the armed services and are not part of the formal court system.

Appeals from the decisions of these federal courts are permitted, but the route of these appeals differs.

- District court cases and Tax Court cases are appealed to the various U.S. courts of appeals;
- Court of International Trade cases and Claims Court cases are appealed only to the U.S. Court of Appeals for the Federal Circuit, located in Washington, D.C.
- Military court cases are appealed to the U.S. Court of Military Appeals.

Further appeals in cases from district court, Tax Court, Claims Court and Court of International Trade may be taken to the Supreme Court, with that Court's permission.

The Intermediate Appeals Courts. A party who loses at the trial level may wish to appeal. The state cannot appeal a "not guilty" verdict in a criminal case and obtain a conviction of the defendant (though in many jurisdictions it can appeal the determination of issues of law for use in future cases and can appeal the length of sentence imposed on a defendant who is convicted), but a defendant in a criminal case can generally appeal a guilty verdict. A defendant who has lost a criminal case and faces prison may believe that improperly obtained evidence was used in the trial. He or she would seek to have the verdict reversed and have the case tried again following the rules. Similarly, someone ordered to pay money because of losing a civil case may well believe that the law was applied incorrectly at trial.

Appeals courts, in the state and federal systems alike, sit to review the procedures of trials held in lower courts. However, it is important to clear up a common misconception about appeals courts. They do *not* retry the cases they hear. They don't hear witnesses and weigh evidence. Instead, the appeal is usually confined to questions of law relating to the facts and the record of the case made at the trial level. The role of appeals courts is to make sure that trial courts have followed the substantive or procedural law correctly. Though their rulings may have an impact upon the interpretation or admissibility of certain facts, appeals courts do not make their own independent search for facts.

If the appeals court decides that the rules were not adhered to, it will not find the defendant innocent. Appeals courts do not impose new verdicts. They don't find defendants guilty or not guilty. Rather, they (1) affirm or reverse the verdict or judgment of the court below, (2) dismiss the appeal (often with the concurrence of the parties), or (3) send the case back to the trial court for a determination of certain facts. If the verdict is affirmed, the loser's usual recourse is to attempt an appeal to a higher court. If the verdict is reversed and remanded, the case is returned to a lower court for retrial. The government will not be able to use the disputed evidence in the new trial, but it might try to convict the defendant using other evidence. Or the appeals court might simply reverse the verdict and return the case to a lower court with orders to dismiss it.

Appeals Courts: State. About three quarters of the states have intermediate appellate courts. The remaining states, which are generally small, have no level of court between trial courts and the highest court in the state.

The right to appeal is not a constitutional right in all circumstances, but state legislatures in the vast majority of jurisdictions have established a right of appeal by law. Intermediate courts of appeals differ in the scope of their jurisdiction.

Appeals Courts: Federal. There are thirteen intermediate courts of appeals in the federal system. Twelve are set up geographically. One of these covers only the District of Columbia; the other eleven cover varying numbers of states. The largest covers nine states, the smallest three. There are 156 judges on these 12 appellate courts. Each court of appeals consists of between six and twenty-eight judges, depending upon the amount of work in the region. The 12 regional courts of appeals receive about 33,000 cases each year. They hear appeals from the district courts, Tax Court, and various federal agencies.

The other intermediate federal court of appeals—the Court of Appeals for the Federal Circuit—has national jurisdiction. Located in Washington, D.C., it has 12 judges and hears appeals in patent law from all district courts, as well as appeals from the United States Claims Court, the United States Court of International Trade, and a number of federal agencies.

A decision in one circuit is not binding on any other; conflicts may be resolved only by the U.S. Supreme Court.

The Highest Courts. At the top of every American court system is the court of last resort, the state "supreme" court. (It is not called that in every state. In New York, for example, the highest court is called the Court of Appeals, and the Supreme Court is actually a trial court.) In all state systems and in the federal system, the highest court has the final authority to interpret the law.

The highest courts of the states may be reversed by the Supreme Court of the United States—but only on matters of federal constitutional or federal statutory interpretation. The U.S. Supreme Court may be overruled only by amendment to the U.S. Constitution, or, of course, by itself.

Highest State Courts. The supreme courts of the 50 states do not conduct trials. Their function is appellate—reviewing the legal procedure and rulings of courts below them.

Generally, these courts, like intermediate courts of appeals, do not disturb or even reconsider the facts of the cases they are reviewing. They exist to review only the law.

State supreme courts have a wide-ranging jurisdiction. They have authority, customarily, to review all types of cases. State supreme courts have as few as three members, but the more common size is either five or seven.

The U. S. Supreme Court. In America, there is only one court created by the U.S. Constitution. It is the Supreme Court of the United States, the only tribunal specifically required by the Constitution. Congress is empowered but not required by the Constitution to create, or abolish, any other federal court.

The Supreme Court is one of the three great branches of the U.S. government. As a co-equal institution with the presidency and Congress, the Court provides a vital function. The Court must interpret and apply the Constitution to cases involving the other branches of government and the states. Chief Justice John Marshall declared, "It is emphatically the province and duty of the judiciary department to say what the law is," and the Court has carried out that duty in deciding whether actions of the executive branch, Congress, the states, and the lower courts are in accord with the Constitution, in order to assure that rights guaranteed to the people by our fundamental law are not abridged.

The types of cases that it may hear on appeal (its appellate jurisdiction) are defined by laws passed by Congress, and over the years, Congress has generally passed laws giving the justices an increasingly wide range of cases for possible review. The Court also has a class of cases which it alone tries—its original jurisdiction—and those are spelled out by the Constitution itself. An example would be a lawsuit filed by one state against another. As a matter of fact, however, the Supreme Court is likely to decide no more than one or two "original" cases in any of its annual terms.

Out of the thousands of cases which the court is asked to review each year, the justices select about 150 cases for full-scale review during each nine-month sitting, or term. Those are the cases it decides, with written opinions, after full briefing and a public oral argument. As with other appellate courts, should they decline to hear a case the effect is to let stand the lower court's ruling.

The Court has nine justices. The figure is set by federal law; over the years, it has ranged from a low of six, at the beginning, to as high as ten, after the Civil War. At least six of the nine justices must participate for the Court to have a quorum to do any business. It takes the votes of only four justices to grant full review of a case.

Lawyers, Judges and the Courts

LAWYERS

The judicial process in America often begins with lawyers and their clients. This booklet hasn't the space to consider guidelines for choosing and using a lawyer. A companion volume in this series, "The American Lawyer," contains a number of considerations that bear on choosing a lawyer and deciding when to proceed with legal action.

Attorneys (and clients) who think first of going to court may be acting, at least in some circumstances, in a way that will do the client no good, and may in fact harm the client's interests. As important as the role of "advocate" is for lawyers, it is no more important than their role as counselors or negotiators. In performing as counselors or negotiators, lawyers may—and often do—find that going to court is not what they would want to do for their client.

In a civil case, the lawyers work for the parties involved in the suit, representing either the plaintiff (the party bringing the suit) or the defendant (the party being sued). In a criminal case, the prosecuting attorney represents the government, while the defense attorney represents his or her client. Those defendants who do not have the money to retain a private attorney have the right to be defended at no charge by a public defender.

Lawyers are not government officials unless, as is the case with city and county attorneys, prosecuting attorneys, and public defenders, they happen to work for the government. Lawyers are, however, "officers of the court." Lawyers and judges are expected to adhere to high standards of ethical conduct. Lawyers are subject to discipline for misconduct, and lawyer disciplinary agencies exist in every state with the authority to investigate charges of lawyer misconduct. If a client believes that a lawyer has engaged in unethical or improper conduct, the client may contact the state's lawyer disciplinary agency. Information concerning the state's lawyer disciplinary agency, such as its address and telephone number, should be obtainable from the state bar association. See "The American Lawyer" for a discussion of legal ethics and professionalism.

JUDGES

Given the usually accepted statistic that few decisions of trial courts are appealed, especially in civil cases, and the fact that most trial court rulings that are appealed are upheld, it is clear that the judge on the trial bench is a key figure of the American judiciary, at least for cases that go to trial and are not settled before being decided by the judge or jury.

The most commonly recognized role of the trial judge is to be the umpire in disputes under the American system of "adversary" justice. Not only is it assumed that the judge as umpire will be neutral, it is the judges's obligation to be neutral.

A significant part of the judge's role is to keep the case in proper legal bounds by ruling on points of law and procedure.

In addition to presiding over trials, judges have many other functions. For example, criminal court judges are responsible for a variety of activities even before a trial begins:

1. they issue arrest and search warrants;
2. they ensure that defendants are informed of the charge(s) and of their right to be represented by counsel;
3. they set and revoke bail;
4. they hold probable-cause hearings to determine if the accused person should be held for trial; and
5. they rule on pre-trial procedural motions (e.g., to exclude certain evidence).

Over the past twenty years, an additional judicial responsibility has been recognized. Whereas the judge's role as impartial umpire was formerly regarded as a limit on the power to control the processing of cases—for example, cases were usually deemed ready for trial only when all the parties were ready to proceed—a growing number of observers now agree that the judge must take responsibility for the movement of cases in order to reduce or eliminate the backlogs and delay that now plague many court systems. For example, standards adopted by the National Conference of State Trial Judges mandate that the judge assume an active role in causing cases to be promptly concluded; a recent report prepared by the American Bar Association's Commission on Professionalism concludes that "The role of the judiciary in the conduct of litigation should be strengthened and courts should play a more decisive role earlier in the litigation process. . . . There is a public interest in not clogging the courts with stale cases." The recommendation of the American Bar Association's Action Commission to Improve the Tort Liability System states that "A 'fast track' system should be adopted for the trial of tort cases. In recommending such a system, we endorse a policy of active judicial management of the pre-trial phases of tort litigation."

Many participants and observers of our court system believe that civil and criminal lawsuits at all levels of courts take too long and cost too much. The Institute for Court Management of the National Center for State Courts, the American Bar Association, and the American Judicature Society are among the many national organizations studying the problems of court cost and delay. The adverse impacts of court delay may be best summarized by the National Conference of State Trial Judges in the Comment that accompanies Standard 2.50 of the Standards relating to Court Delay Reduction, which reads, in part, as follows:

> . . . Delay devalues judgments, creates anxiety in litigants, and results in loss or deterioration of the evidence upon which rights are determined. Accumulated delay produces backlogs that waste court resources, needlessly increase lawyer fees, and create confusion and conflict in allocating judges' time. The public expects and deserves prompt and affordable justice. . . .

Active caseflow management has proven to be one successful technique for reducing court costs and delay, without sacrificing the procedures and protections of the law. Caseflow management requires (1) continuous court control of the pace of litigation beginning with the time cases are first filed in the court, (2) time standards for completion of significant events within the case and overall, (3) monitoring of intermediate events within the court process to ensure that they are completed on time, and (4) the commitment by participants that trials and hearings will occur when scheduled.

Individual trial courts and entire state trial court systems have adopted caseflow management techniques to reduce court cost and delay. A 1986 survey conducted by the Conference of State Court Administrators indicates that twenty-two states now have statewide trial court time standards. Eleven more states have time standards in effect in local trial courts.

While initially the national emphasis in cost and delay reduction programs was at the trial court level, appellate courts have also taken steps to reduce the time required to complete cases. Preliminary results from the 1987 State Court Administrators survey suggest that almost half of those responding consider appellate court delay a serious problem. The Appellate Judges Conference of the American Bar Association is developing new appellate standards encouraging the use of caseflow management and establishing national time standards as benchmarks for appellate courts.

Court-annexed mediation and arbitration of civil cases is often included in trial court cost and delay reduction programs. Mediation is also used in appellate courts. Caseflow management and the various alternative dispute resolution mechanisms are intended to respond to the public's desire that tax dollars be spent in the most efficient manner. Their goal is to allow judicial institutions to provide increased service without substantially increased resources. They seek to shorten the time in which cases are settled. And since over 90 percent of civil cases are settled—never decided by a court—that would be a considerable accomplishment.

The Trial Judge. When a judge tries a case without a jury, which may occur in civil and minor criminal cases more often than in criminal cases involving a felony, he or she is the sole "fact-finder." It is the judge who listens to the evidence and decides what facts the evidence has established, and the inferences to be drawn from those facts, that together form the basis for the legal judgment.

When cases are tried before a jury, the judge still has a major role in determining which evidence may be considered by the jury. The jury is the fact-finder, but it is left to "find" facts only from the evidence which is legally admissible. The judge makes rulings, based on law, about which evidence may be presented to the jury and which may not be. Moreover, the judge can have a profound influence over jury's deliberation by the instructions he or she gives to the jury on the legal principles or rules that must be followed in weighing the facts.

The Appellate Judge/Supreme Court Justice. The facts that emerge from a trial court are usually beyond review or challenge in appellate or supreme courts. Appeals concern the application of the law that governed a verdict, not the facts upon which it was based.

The role of the appellate judge, then, is almost exclusively one of legal interpretation. He or she sits primarily to review and, if necessary, to correct the judgments in law and procedure made by the trial judge.

SELECTING, EVALUATING, AND DISCIPLINING JUDGES

Methods of Selection. Some judges in this country are appointed, some are elected. Methods of selection vary considerably among the states, and between the states and the federal government.

All federal judges are appointed. For judges authorized under Article III of the Constitution, nominations are made by the president, and the Senate accepts or rejects the nominees. These appointments are for life, except in very rare instances of misconduct severe enough to result in impeachment.

States are free to select their own way of choosing judges. Most states require judges to be lawyers, but some do not. Some state judges are appointed; some are elected. In some states a mixed system is in effect, with judges appointed initially but retained in office only if they succeed in a retention election.

In two-thirds of the states and the District of Columbia, some or all judges are selected under the merit selection system. The merit system originated in Missouri, and is sometimes referred to as "The Missouri Plan." Merit selection is a way of choosing judges that uses a permanent, non-partisan commission of lawyers and non-lawyers—usually composed of public officials, attorneys and private citizens—to locate, recruit, investigate and evaluate applicants for judgeships. The commission then submits the names of the most highly qualified applicants (usually three) to the appointing authority (usually the governor), who must make a final selection from the list. For subsequent terms of office, judges are evaluated for retention either by a commission or by the voters.

Here are the forms of judicial selection in use in the states

APPOINTMENT:

- nominated by a merit-screening panel and appointed by another official or entity;
- nominated by a governor or some other executive officer, state or local, subject to legislative confirmation;
- nominated and appointed by the governor or other executive, with no legislative review;
- nominated and appointed by the state legislature or by a local legislative body;
- nominated and appointed by the state supreme court or by other state judges.

ELECTION:

- nominated by partisan organizations or conventions, with popular election in general elections;
- nominated by party primary election, elected by general election;
- nominated in non-partisan primaries, elected by non-partisan general election.

MIXED SYSTEM:

- initial appointment as above; to be continued in office after initial term, the judge must be retained by popular vote in a special judicial retention election. Usually, judges seeking retention have no opposition, but have to receive a certain percentage of the votes cast in the judicial contest (usually 50 percent or 60 percent) to be retained. If they fail to be retained, their positions are declared vacant and new judges are appointed.

Evaluating Judges. A number of state courts have recently begun evaluation programs primarily for the self-improvement of judges and the judiciary. These programs assist judges in improving their on-the-bench performance by giving them specific feedback from people who have appeared before them, including attorneys, jurors, litigants, and other appropriate sources.

Beginning in 1983, the American Bar Association's Special Committee on Evaluation of Judicial Performance developed guidelines to assist state courts in developing appropriate programs.

In providing judges with meaningful performance feedback, the ABA guidelines urge use of carefully designed questionnaires which are completed by only those who have personal and current knowledge of a judge's performance.

The highest court with the administrative responsibility for the court system (often the state supreme court) is responsible for developing and implementing the program. The supreme courts in Connecticut, New Jersey, and Vermont are now successfully implementing such programs. In Alaska, performance evaluations are conducted primarily to give voters information on the performance of judges to assist them in making an informed decision about judges who are up for retention election. Planning committees in Colorado, Delaware, Illinois, Puerto Rico, Utah, and Washington state are developing evaluation programs using the ABA guidelines.

Disciplining Judges. No matter how judges are selected at any level of government, they are subject to discipline for serious misconduct, on or off the bench.

Federal judges may be disciplined by impeachment (filing of formal charges, followed by legislative trial, with removal from the bench upon conviction), or by lesser sanctions, such as reprimand by the chief judge of the circuit and removal of all work (but not of salary).

During the 1960s and 1970s, there was a major movement toward new methods of disciplining state judges. Every state (and the District of Columbia) now has, by constitution, statute, or court rule, a judicial discipline mechanism using some form of commission. The commission (which may be known by other names in various states, such as board or committee) may be composed of (1) judges; (2) judges and lawyers; (3) judges, lawyers, and lay persons; or (4) lawyers and lay people. The commission has authority to investigate complaints against judges. Complaints could range from the trivial to serious misconduct or physical or mental incapacity. The most common ground for complaint is "conduct prejudicial to the administration of justice." Others include "willful misconduct" and "violation of the Code of Judicial Conduct," which was promulgated by the American Bar Association in 1972 and adopted by some states in the intervening years. The Code established rules for the conduct of judges, covering such topics as their behavior on the bench, their involvement in politics, possible conflicts with their judicial duties, and business dealings that conflict with judicial independence.

The commissions are authorized to recommend to the state's highest court such sanctions as the use of punishment short of removal from office—including public or private reprimand, censure, and suspension—as well as involuntary retirement and removal.

State judges also still may face the older forms of judicial discipline, such as impeachment, or the process known as "address" (filing of formal charges, followed by legislative trial, with request for dismissal by the executive), or recall (a summons to go before the voters in a special election to determine whether the judge should be removed from office). However, these mechanisms have fallen into disuse in most states.

Disciplinary systems vary from state to state, but all have a common thread: anyone who has knowledge of possible misconduct by a judge has the right to report the judge's behavior to an agency charged with regulating judges' conduct.

COURTROOM DESIGN: ALTERNATIVE #1

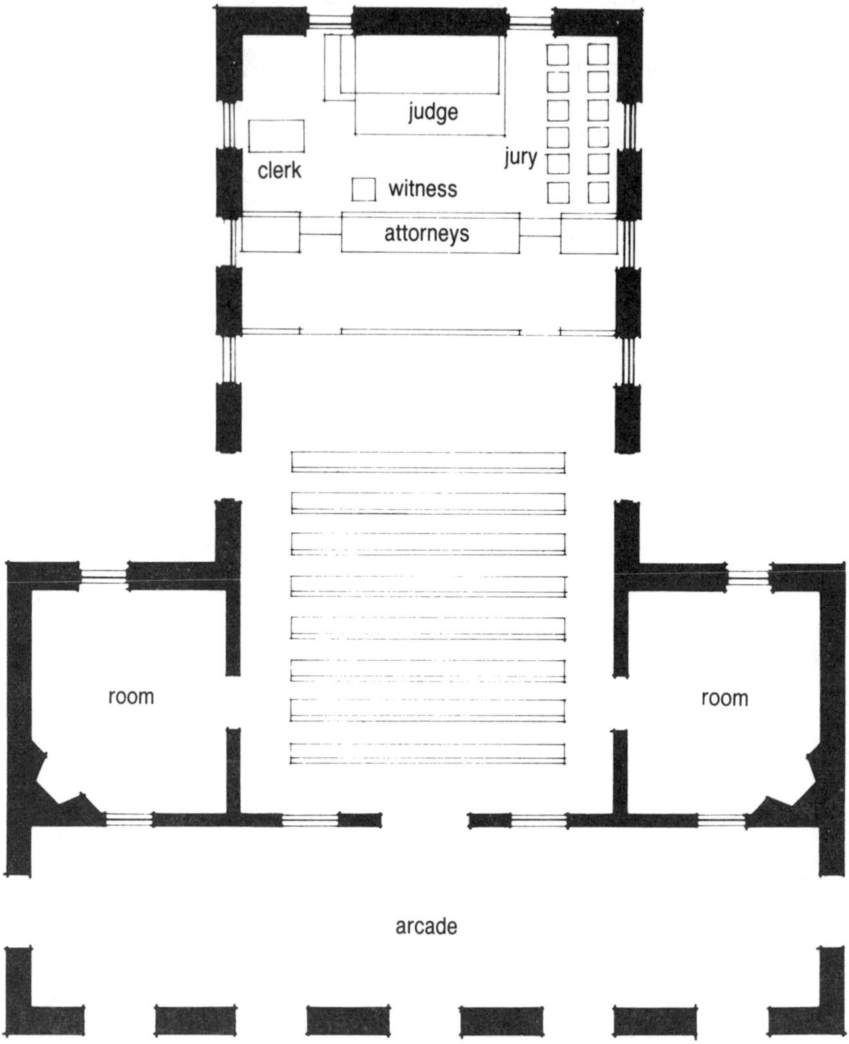

This T-shaped plan with judge's bench at the base of the T is typical of the colonial period. Small conference/jury rooms open from each side.

Special Tribunals

Every lawsuit in America is, in its own way, special—if for no other reason than the different facts in each. But in some jurisdictions certain legal actions have become the special province of tribunals created just to process those kind of cases.

Some of these tribunals were created because of the type of matters which come before them. It was thought that the special conditions of these matters, and the expertise that these matters require, called for special courts. That is true, for example, of courts for juveniles who get into trouble, or for married couples contemplating separation or divorce. It is also true of disciplinary panels for lawyers or commissions on judicial conduct.

Some tribunals exist to deal with a single branch of the law. An example is the probate court, or orphans' court, which administers estates, either where there is a will or where there is not.

Some courts are created solely to handle lawsuits for money damages against the federal or state government. These are the "claims" courts.

Some courts come into being to handle simple and low-value money or property disputes between private parties. An example would be a "small claims" court.

COURTS OF SPECIAL JURISDICTION

In some states, the functions discussed below are handled by courts specially created for that purpose. In other states—and they are the majority—these functions are handled within the regular trial courts established by law—courts of limited or general jurisdiction—though often by branches of these courts which specialize in these matters.

Family Courts. Where they exist, family courts are part of a state court system. There are no family courts in the federal system. The best known branches of family law are domestic relations—divorce, marital separation, child custody—and in some states problems of juveniles. (In some states, juvenile problems are handled by juvenile courts.)

Proceedings in family courts will usually emphasize negotiations, reconciliation, and conciliation in order to try to avert more serious difficulty. However, family courts will also have available trial-type procedures for use if disputes cannot be resolved. The rules of civil trial procedure usually will be followed. Family courts do not generally use juries; their proceedings are most often before judges alone.

In addressing issues of domestic relations, family courts are empowered not only to arrange or supervise separation agreements, but also to grant divorces. In granting decrees of divorce, the courts will customarily divide assets and liabilities, make awards of alimony and child support, and award child custody.

In confronting problems of juveniles, family and juvenile courts may seek to rely upon highly informal advisory or counseling sessions, or may use more formal procedures that will have some of the aspects of a criminal trial. In some jurisdictions, these courts are empowered to issue orders requiring that older juveniles be tried as adults in regular criminal courts.

Judgments of family or juvenile courts in juvenile cases may actually lead to forms of confinement in specialized institutions, but their stated purpose is to provide treatment rather than punishment.

Proceedings regarding juveniles customarily are not open to the public, in order to protect juvenile reputations. Divorce proceedings and other family court proceedings are often open to the public.

Probate Courts. Special courts to administer estates exist in a few states. They are known by such names as probate courts or orphans' courts or surrogate courts. In other states these matters are handled by general or limited jurisdiction courts. It is their task to interpret last wills in the event of uncertainty or conflict over the will's meaning, or to determine rights to an estate (where the deceased person has died "intestate," or without a will). Probate courts supervise the distribution of estates. Probate courts demonstrate one of the most important purposes of courts in our society—they make a formal record of legal status of property. Procedures in probate courts may be very brief or summary in form (as when wills are self-executing, and the probate court need only review them briefly to determine their legal sufficiency and authenticity) or the procedures may develop into full-scale adversary proceedings. Probate courts are usually judge-only tribunals, though jury trials may be available for adversary proceedings.

Claims Courts. In a few states, and at the federal level, special tribunals are authorized to hear and determine claims for money damages against government agencies. (In most states, these claims are heard by general or limited jurisdiction courts.)

They are a form of civil court that, by use of conventional procedures, will determine whether a person or company doing business with the government, or a person employed by government, or a person whose property is damaged by the government (e.g., as in an accident with a government vehicle), has been wronged in that relationship, and is entitled to recover damages.

Small Claims Courts. Separate small claims courts exist in a few states. Generally, small claims are handled by general or limited jurisdiction courts applying special procedures. A handful of states have no small claims procedures.

Generally, a small claims court is a miniature, or simplified, civil court, with jurisdiction limited to amounts under a figure set by law. Usually the amount in dispute is not enough to require the full panoply of formal court procedures. Small claims courts save people the expense of a regular civil lawsuit. The claim may involve a dispute over money or over property, provided that the amount in dispute is below a specified figure.

These courts usually are conducted without attorneys for either side. (For this reason, they are sometimes known as "pro se," courts, from the Latin phrase meaning "for oneself.") The judge, acting alone, will seek to determine whether there is a just claim, and if so, how much it is to be. The process is usually highly informal. Usually decisions cannot be appealed in a higher court.

The popular TV program "The People's Court" is an example of the informal, quick justice provided by small claims courts.

Other Specialized Courts. A few states have established workers' compensation courts, and tax courts exist in a handful of states.

Administrative Tribunals. Many, if not most, regulatory agencies have tribunals that function somewhat like courts in that they apply the policies of the agency on a case-by-case basis.

Administrative tribunals include: labor arbitration panels, lawyer disciplinary committees or panels, and commissions on judicial conduct. But the variety stretches much further: it includes state public utility commissions; medical, architectural and pharmacological licensing boards; contract administration boards; civil service review boards; and an array of federal agencies: the National Labor Relations Board, the Federal Power Commission, Federal Trade Commission, Federal Election Commission, Federal Communications Commission, Federal Aviation Agency, Federal Railroad Administration, Interstate Commerce Commission, Civil Aeronautics Board, Federal Maritime Commission, and on and on.

The function of the agencies is, more often than not, split between the fashioning of specific regulations, and the implementation of those regulations on a case-by-case basis. Thus, they are quasi-legislative, quasi-judicial, and quasi-executive.

Generally speaking, cases will be handled much as civil cases in court would be. Normal rules of evidence, or something akin to that, will be followed. The proceeding often will be an "adversary" one, with two distinct sides seeking to win.

The Constitution's guarantee of "due process" must be observed as faithfully by regulators as by judges. Generally speaking, this means that an agency may not take away or deny a privilege or impose a sanction without first giving the person or institution involved notice that it may happen, and then an opportunity to offer reasons why it should not happen.

Court Procedures

This section is based on the Federal Rules of Civil Procedure and the Federal Rules of Criminal Procedure, which are in effect in the federal courts and are the basis for the rules followed in many state courts. These rules are to make the trial process simple and fair. (Note, however, that these rules are not in effect in every state court system. The states differ in their procedures, and the generalizations we make below might not apply in their entirety to your state's courts. Moreover, the procedures in a given state may change. The best source for up-to-date information is the state bar association or the state court administrator, located in the state capital, with offices in some states in the larger cities as well.)

In civil cases the process begins with the filing of a complaint, to which the other side files an answer. The side filing the suit may then have to file a reply.

It is not necessary for a complaint to be prepared with technical precision to conform to the law. It is supposed to be simply a concise statement of the claim against the other party, to put the party on notice of the action. The answer admits or denies the allegations made in the complaint. The reply gives the person filing the complaint an opportunity to respond to new matters raised by the defendant's answer. Motions can be made to clarify these documents or to ask that the lawsuit be dismissed before it comes to trial, and for other purposes, such as to discover evidence.

The rules are similarly simple in criminal cases. A crime is charged by an indictment filed by a grand jury or by a complaint or by a document called an "information" filed by the prosecutor in states that do not routinely use the grand jury to bring charges. The defendant is allowed to plead guilty, not guilty, or, if the court grants its permission, no contest (nolo contendere). Motions are available to the defendant to ask that the charges be clarified or dismissed.

By adopting the federal rules, many states have allowed lawyers to follow the same procedures in both state and federal court.

PRE-TRIAL PROCEDURES IN CIVIL CASES

This section on pre-trial procedure deals with a typical civil case that proceeds to trial. However, because most civil suits are settled without a court decision, it is important first to discuss civil case settlements.

Settlement. Very few lawsuits ever go to trial. They are settled by mutual agreement between the parties. A dispute can be settled even before a suit is filed. Once a suit is filed, it can be settled before the trial begins, during the trial, while the jury is deliberating, or even after a verdict is rendered.

A settlement does not usually state that anyone was right or wrong in the case, nor does it have to settle the whole case. Part of a dispute can be settled, with the remaining issues left to be resolved by the court.

A settlement can take many forms. It can rest on certain conditions (that the aggrieved party gets his or her job back, or that he or she experiences no permanent disability from an injury, for example). It can be oral or written, although a written settlement is always preferable. The only thing needed for a settlement is the agreement of all parties.

Settlements are encouraged, and devices such as court-ordered arbitration and other forms of alternative dispute resolution (see below) provide mechanisms for resolving disputes outside of the formal court system.

Alternative Dispute Resolution. Alternatives to the traditional court process take many forms. They usually involve impartial decision-makers such as mediators or arbitrators. Alternative dispute resolution is rapidly growing, as the following figures suggest:

Number of	*1977*	*1986*
Mediation Programs	100	360
Community Mediators	5,000	20,000
Jurisdictions Requiring Mediation	0	33
Bar Association Alternative Dispute Resolution Committees	0	100

Alternative dispute resolution is not a new concept in the judicial system. Most civil cases are settled before going to trial by using a variety of techniques to bring about voluntary settlements, including pre-trial settlement conferences, mediation by magistrates, court-annexed arbitration, and, at times, mediation in chambers by the judge.

In at least 20 states, court-annexed arbitration or mediation is automatic for many cases. In court-annexed arbitration or mediation, certain cases—for example, those under a certain dollar amount—*must* initially be sent to arbitration or mediation. However, sometimes the losing party in arbitration or mediation may appeal, which sends the case back into the court system. In some states a party has a right to a new trial (*trial de novo*) before a judge and jury. Sometimes there is a requirement that the result of the trial improve the position of the party by a certain percentage (often 10 percent) or the party will have to pay court costs.

Other communities have experimental programs for removing some cases from the courts and deciding them through arbitration or mediation in places such as neighborhood justice centers.

Arbitration is widely used in commercial, insurance and labor-management disagreements. It involves submitting the dispute to a third party who renders a decision after hearing arguments and reviewing evidence. It may be less formal, less complex, less costly, and often can be concluded more quickly than court proceedings. In its most common form—binding arbitration—the parties select the arbitrator and are bound by the decision, either by prior agreement or by statute. In last-offer arbitration, the arbitrator is required to choose between the final positions of the two parties.

Conciliation is an informal process in which the third party tries to lower tensions, improve communications, interpret issues, provide technical assistance, explore potential solutions and bring about a negotiated settlement, either informally, or, in a subsequent step, through formal mediation. Conciliation is frequently used in volatile conflicts and in disputes where the parties are unable or unwilling to come to the table to negotiate their differences.

Mediation is a bit more structured process in which a third-party mediator assists the disputants to reach a negotiated settlement of their differences. Mediation is usually a voluntary process that results in a signed agreement which spells out the terms of the settlement and defines the future behavior of the parties. The mediator uses a variety of skills and techniques to help the parties reach a settlement but is not empowered to render a decision.

Med-Arb is an innovation in dispute resolution under which the med-arbiter is authorized by the parties to serve first as a mediator and, secondly, as an arbitrator empowered to decide any issues not resolved through mediation.

Neighborhood Justice Centers (NJC) now exist in many localities throughout the country, under the sponsorship of local or state governments, bar associations, and foundations. NJCs primarily resolve disputes between individuals with ongoing relationships (landlord-tenant, husband-wife, neighbors, etc.). Many draw their caseloads from referrals from police, local courts or prosecutors' offices with which they are affiliated. The dispute resolution techniques most often offered by the centers are mediation and conciliation.

How Does a Lawsuit Begin? While settlements account for the resolutions of the vast majority of the civil suits filed, very often they occur after a complaint has been filed and some procedures undertaken in the court system. And of course the remaining cases do go to trial. For all these reasons, it's important that the steps in a trial be clear to a layperson.

An aggrieved person becomes a plaintiff if he or she—or a lawyer representing the person—prepares and files a *complaint* in the proper court. The person or firm against whom the case is filed is the *defendant*.

The complaint states the plaintiff's version of the facts, the legal theory under which the case is brought (negligence, for example), and asks for certain damages or other relief. The plaintiff also files with the court clerk a request that a *summons* (or notice) be issued to the defendant. In many jurisdictions, the summons will be served by a deputy sheriff or special process server. In some states, it may be served by mail. It notifies the defendant that a lawsuit has been filed against him or her.

After being notified, the defendant has a certain period of time to file an *answer*. This time period is 20 days in federal courts and varies from state to state in state courts.

Jurisdiction and Venue. The plaintiff's lawyer must decide where to file the case. A court has no authority to decide a case unless it has *jurisdiction* over the person or property involved. To have jurisdiction, a court must have authority over the subject matter of the case and be able to exercise control over the defendant, or the property involved must be located in the area under the court's control. The extent of the court's control over persons and property is set by statute, and is explained or clarified by decisions of the state's highest appellate court in actual cases.

Certain actions are *transitory*. They can be brought in any county in any state where the defendant may be found and served with a summons and the jurisdiction has sufficient contact with one of the parties and the incident which gave rise to the suit. Other actions are *local*. They can be brought only in the county where the subject of a suit is located. An example of the latter is a lawsuit for the foreclosure of a mortgage on real estate.

Venue refers to the county or district within a state or the United States where the lawsuit is to be tried. The venue of a lawsuit is set by statute. Venue may be changed to another county or district in some cases. If a case has received widespread pre-trial publicity, a motion for a change of venue may be granted by the judge in an effort to secure jurors who have not already formed an opinion about the case. Venue also may be changed for the convenience of witnesses.

Pleadings. Pleadings are certain formal documents filed with the court that state the parties' basic positions. They should not be confused with the arguments made in court by the lawyers. Common pre-trial pleadings include the following:

Complaint (or *petition* or *bill*). Probably the most important pleading in the case, since by setting out the plaintiff's version of the facts and specifying the damages, it frames the issues of the case.

Answer. This statement by the defendant responds to the allegations in the plaintiff's complaint. It is a statement by the defendant explaining why the plaintiff should not prevail. It may also offer additional facts, or plead an excuse.

Reply. Any party in the case may have to file a reply, which is an answer to new allegations raised by the other party or parties in prior pleadings.

Counterclaim. Through a counterclaim, the defendant sues for relief or damages from the plaintiff, and perhaps others. ("You're suing me? Well then, I'm suing you.") It may be filed separately or as part of the answer. If a counterclaim is filed, the plaintiff in turn may file any of the motions below in answer to the counterclaim.

Motions. Motions are not pleadings but are requests for the judge to make a legal ruling. During a trial, lawyers will make various types of motions relating to the admissibility of evidence and the like. Similarly, before the trial certain kinds of legal questions require a determination. The following are some of the most common pre-trial motions:

Motion for Summary Judgment. This motion asks the court for a judgment on the merits of the case *before* the trial. It is often made where there is no dispute about the facts and only a question of law needs to be decided.

Motion to Discover. A common pre-trial motion by which one party seeks to gain information held by the adverse party. (See below.)

Motion to Dismiss. This motion asks the court to dismiss the suit because the suit does not have a legally sound basis, even if all the facts alleged are proven true.

Other, less common, pre-trial motions include:

Motion to Quash Service of Summons. This motion seeks dismissal of the lawsuit on the grounds that the defendant was not properly served with the summons. There are many other motions to quash. For example, the defense in a criminal case may make a motion to quash (suppress) evidence which it believes has been illegally obtained.

Motion to Strike. This motion asks the court to strike from the plaintiff's petition irrelevant, prejudicial or other improper material. The court may order that offending passages be removed.

Motion to Make More Definite or Certain. This motion asks the court to require the plaintiff to state the facts of the case more specifically, or to describe the injuries or damages more clearly.

Discovery. To begin preparing for trial, both sides engage in discovery. That is the formal process of exchanging information between the parties to find out information relevant to witnesses and other evidence each side will present at trial.

Discovery enables the litigants to know before the trial begins what facts may be presented. It is designed to prevent "trial by ambush," where evidence or witnesses are discovered by the opposing party only when presented at the trial, with no time to marshal answering evidence.

The most common method of discovery is the taking of depositions. A *deposition* is an out-of-court statement given under oath by a witness to be used at trial or in preparation for trial. In most states, either of the parties may take the deposition of the other party, or of any other witness. Both sides have the right to be present during oral depositions.

Depositions are taken to enable a party to know in advance what a witness will say at the trial. Depositions also may be taken to obtain the testimony of important witnesses who cannot appear during the trial. In such a case, the deposition may be read into evidence at the trial.

Often a witness's deposition will be taken by the opposing side and used to discredit the witness's testimony at trial when the trial testimony varies from the testimony taken during the deposition.

Usually depositions consist of an oral examination, followed by cross-examination by the opposing side. In addition to taking depositions, either party may submit written questions, called *interrogatories*, to the other party and require that they be answered in writing under oath.

In many jurisdictions, discovery requests do not have to go before a judge, unless the parties have a dispute over the relevency of questions or some other matter pertaining to the depositions. If discovery requests are brought before a judge, he or she will approve them as long as they are relevant to the case or do not seek privileged information—that is, discussions between spouses or between lawyer and client, priest and penitent, or doctor and patient that are legally protected from disclosure. A judge may prevent discovery if one side is using it not as a means of discovering specific evidence, but instead to annoy or embarrass the other side or as a "fishing expedition" to search for information.

Other methods of discovery include subpoenaing or requiring the other side to produce books, records or other documents for inspection; having the other side submit to a physical examination; or asking that a document be submitted for examination to determine if it is genuine.

Pre-Trial Conference. Courts use conferences with counsel for many purposes. One type of pre-trial conference gaining in popularity is the *status conference* (sometimes called the "early conference"). This conference is often the primary device used for establishing judicial control of the case. Held after all initial pleadings have been filed, this conference is used to establish times within which all pre-trial activities are to be concluded. A tentative trial date may be set. If the court uses court-annexed alternative dispute resolution, reference to the ADR program may be made at this hearing.

Another important purpose of pre-trial conferences is to encourage the settlement of cases. The conference provides an opportunity for the judge and the lawyers to review the evidence and clarify the issues in dispute.

If a case has not been settled, many courts set a time for an *issue conference*. The lawyers usually appear at this hearing before a judge without their clients and try to agree on undisputed facts or points of law. Such agreements are called *stipulations*. The issue conference can shorten the actual trial time by determining points that do not need to be proved during the trial.

If a settlement does not take place through pre-trial conferences, the judge sets a date for the trial.

PRE-TRIAL PROCEDURES IN CRIMINAL CASES

Pre-trial procedures in criminal cases follow the general pattern established in civil cases, but with important variations.

Bringing the Charge. Criminal charges are brought against a person in one of three ways:

1. Through an *indictment* voted by a grand jury.
2. Through the filing of an *information* by the prosecuting attorney (also called the county, district, or state's attorney) alleging that a crime was committed. Sometimes charges are pressed through the filing of a criminal *complaint* by another individual, which is essentially a petition to the district attorney asking him/her to initiate charges.
3. Through a *citation* by a police officer for minor traffic offenses and the like. This procedure is usually used for certain *misdemeanors* and other minor criminal matters.

The charge must tell the time, date and place that the criminal act allegedly took place, the alleged involvement of the accused, and the details of the crime itself.

The Grand Jury. Grand juries exist in the federal system but are used in only about half the states. Where the grand jury is used in the states, its function is often limited to investigating public corruption or such tasks as monitoring conditions in the jail.

The grand jury is a body of citizens, varying in size from state to state, summoned by the court. In the federal system and in the states in which it still serves its traditional function in criminal cases, its role is to determine whether and against whom criminal charges should be filed. If a grand jury finds sufficient evidence that a person has committed a crime, it then issues an indictment against that person. In states without grand juries, or states whose grand juries primarily investigate public corruption, charges are brought by the prosecutor's filing an information against the defendant.

Grand jury proceedings are secret. The public, the news media, and the person being investigated have no right to be present. In most jurisdictions, people called to testify before a grand jury are not allowed to be represented by counsel when appearing before a grand jury. The secrecy of the proceedings is intended to encourage witnesses to speak freely without fear of retaliation, and to protect the persons being investigated in the event that the evidence is deemed insufficient and an indictment is not issued.

The purpose of the grand jury is not to decide the guilt or innocence of a person. It is, instead, to determine whether there is sufficient evidence to bring a person to trial. If people are indicted, they have the opportunity to defend themselves at the ensuing trial. The judge or jury at trial will determine whether a person is "guilty" of the charges.

The grand jury has broad investigative powers. It may compel witnesses to appear and answer questions or submit records.

In addition to investigating possible criminal behavior, when public corruption is alleged a grand jury may conduct an investigation. Besides issuing indictments alleging that a person has committed a crime, a grand jury also may issue a *presentment* detailing the results of its investigation.

In many states it is a crime to reveal information about a grand jury's proceedings. However, witnesses before a federal grand jury are free to describe their testimony after leaving the grand jury room.

Arrest Procedure. When an indictment is returned by a grand jury or an information is filed by the prosecutor, the court clerk issues a *warrant* for the arrest of the persons charged, if they have not already been arrested, and they are taken into custody. (Sometimes, for less serious offenses that don't entail arraignments, defendants are issued citations rather than being arrested.)

When people are arrested, they must be informed that they have the right to remain silent and the right to consult with a lawyer, and that if they cannot afford a lawyer one will be appointed to represent them. They are also warned that anything they say may be held against them. These are often referred to as the *Miranda rights* because the U. S. Supreme Court ruled in 1965 in *Miranda v. Arizona* that when law enforcement officers question people taken into custody, the evidence garnered from their interview cannot be used against them unless they have been informed of their constitutional rights to counsel and to remain silent.

Many states permit law enforcement officials to hold suspects for up to 24 hours without filing a formal charge. Within that time charges must be filed against them or they must be released.

Initial Appearance. Unless the accused persons waive their right to an initial appearance before a judge, one will be scheduled soon after their arrest. (In many jurisdictions this hearing is called a *first* or *initial appearance*. In other jurisdictions it is called a *preliminary hearing* or *arraignment*, though these terms are more usually reserved for a later stage of the criminal justice process.)

This procedure is used for defendants who were not indicted by a grand jury, and serves some of the functions of the grand jury, in that the judge determines whether there was sufficient evidence to charge them with committing a crime. Another purpose of the initial appearance is to ensure that defendants are informed of the charges against them and know their legal rights.

At this hearing the state must demonstrate to a judge that there is sufficient evidence, or *probable cause*, to believe the accused persons committed the crime with which they are charged. The accused persons must be present at this hearing, although they generally do not present evidence in their defense.

A judge might conclude that the state does not have sufficient evidence to support the charges and order the charges dismissed. If this happens the accused persons are released.

If the judge believes the evidence is sufficient, in most cases he or she will set the amount of the defendant's *bail.* This is the amount of money accused persons must post in order to be released from custody until their trial. The purpose of bail is to ensure that the accused will appear for trial. Bail is not supposed to be used as punishment. The bail is returned to defendants when their trial is over, in some states minus a processing fee.

The type of crime alleged, the "dangerousness" of the accused, and the safety of the community are also legitimate issues in the setting of bail. Sometimes bail is conditioned on certain behavior of the accused—for example, that he or she have no contact with the alleged victim.

If defendants are unable to come up with the entire amount of the bail, they may make arrangements for their release through a bail bondsman. In return for the defendant's putting up a percentage of the total bond, usually 10 percent, the bondsman will guarantee the remaining amount to the court should the defendant not be present for trial. In many jurisdictions bondsman are becoming obsolete because courts themselves are releasing defendants upon their payment of 10 percent of the bail to the court.

The judge may release defendants on their *own recognizance*, on the promise that they will appear for all hearings and for trial. This is usually done if defendants have a steady job, roots in the community, or other personal circumstances indicating that they will not flee.

At the initial appearance, the judge will also determine if the accused persons have legal representation. If they cannot afford to hire a lawyer, the court will appoint a public defender, or in some cases a lawyer in private practice, to represent them at public expense.

Arraignment. Most criminal cases are then set for arraignment. When defendants appear for arraignment, the indictment or information is read to them, their rights are explained and they enter their plea. (In some jurisdictions, this procedure may be called a *preliminary hearing*. In these jurisdictions, the defendant's earlier appearance—at which a judge has determined whether there is sufficient evidence to hold him or her—is called a *first* or *initial appearance*.)

If they plead not guilty, a trial date will be set. If they plead guilty, a date will be set for sentencing, although probation, fines or other sentences will be determined immediately for some minor crimes.

In some cases a defendant may be allowed by the judge to plead *nolo contendere*, or no contest. In many jurisdictions a plea of no contest is equivalent to a guilty plea, except that the defendant does not directly admit guilt.

Plea Bargaining. Just as most civil cases are settled before they come to trial, many if not most criminal cases are resolved out of court by having both sides come to an agreement. This process is known as negotiating a plea or plea bargaining. In most jurisdictions it resolves a great majority of the criminal cases filed.

While figures on plea bargaining are hard to come by, some indication of how widespread it is can be garnered from studies that show that the vast majority of criminal convictions result from guilty pleas rather than trial. In 1981, the Bureau of Justice Statistics studied a wide variety of local jurisdictions. Their research showed that over 90 percent of convictions resulted from guilty pleas. A study of federal criminal defendants in the fiscal year ending June 30, 1985, came up with similar findings. Of the more than 38,000 defendants who were convicted, fewer than 5,000 (or less than 15 percent) were convicted at trial. The rest pled guilty.

Plea bargaining is prevalent for practical reasons. Defendants can avoid the time and cost of defending themselves at trial, the risk of harsher punishment, and the publicity a trial could involve. The prosecution saves the time and expense of a lengthy trial. The process resolves both sides' doubts about prevailing. The court system generally is relieved of the burden of conducting a trial on every crime charged.

Plea bargaining usually involves the defendant's pleading guilty to a lesser charge, or to only one of several charges. It also may involve a guilty plea as charged, with the prosecution recommending leniency in sentencing. Many plea bargains are subject to the approval of the court, but many are not (e.g., prosecutors can drop charges without court approval in exchange for a "guilty" plea to a lesser offense).

Plea bargaining is essentially a private process, but this may change now that victims rights groups are more active. Usually the details of a plea bargain are not known publicly until announced in court.

Other alternatives are also possible in the criminal justice system. Many states encourage *diversion* programs which remove less serious criminal matters from the full, formal procedures of the justice system. Typically, the defendant will be allowed to consent to probation without having to go through a trial. If he or she successfully completes the probation—e.g., undergoes rehabilitation or makes restitution for the crime—the matter will be expunged from the records.

Discovery. Discovery is available in criminal cases in some jurisdictions. In many of those jurisdictions both the prosecution and the defense will engage in discovery. Both sides must reveal to each other all witnesses they intend to call to testify at the trial. The prosecution also must reveal all other evidence it will attempt to introduce against the defendant. Some jurisdictions only allow the defense to ask information from the prosecution.

Depositions and *interrogatories* are very rare in criminal cases. Where they exist, they are conducted in the same manner as in civil cases, except that defendants may not be compelled to give testimony against themselves.

TRIALS: CIVIL AND CRIMINAL

While there are some differences in civil and criminal trials, the basic courtroom procedure is the same. This section discusses civil and criminal trial procedure collectively, noting the differences where they occur.

Officers of the Court. The *judge* presides in the courtroom. If a case is tried before a jury, the judge rules on points of law and gives instructions to the jury, informing the jury about the law which governs the case. If there is no jury, the judge determines the facts and decides the verdict—e.g., a finding of guilty or not guilty in a criminal case, or a finding for or against the plaintiff or defendant in a civil trial.

The *court clerk* or *bailiff* usually administers the oath to prospective jurors and to witnesses. The clerk is also the repository of physical exhibits introduced into evidence and is responsible for other administrative aspects of a trial.

The *bailiff* keeps order in the courtroom, calls the witnesses and leads the jury in and out of the courtroom as directed by the judge. It is the bailiff's duty to be certain no one outside the courtroom attempts to influence the jury.

The *court reporter* records everything that is said as part of the formal proceedings in the courtroom, including the testimony of the witnesses, objections made by the lawyers and the judge's rulings on those objections. In a few jurisdictions court reporters are being phased out because audio or audio-visual tapes are serving to record the trial.

The *lawyers* for both sides are also officers of the court. Their job is to represent their clients zealously on the premise that justice can best be achieved if the arguments of each side are vigorously presented by competent legal counsel.

The Jury. The trial jury in either a civil or criminal case is chosen at random from a list called a *venire* or jury pool and compiled by the court clerk. The method of selecting names for the venire varies. In many states the list is compiled from voter registration lists, drivers license lists, or tax assessment rolls. In the federal courts, the court clerk compiles the jury list from the roster of registered voters in the counties comprising the court's jurisdiction. This list is compiled with the assistance of a jury commissioner who is appointed by the presiding judge.

Most states require that a court official screen the list of potential jurors to eliminate persons unqualified or ineligible under relevant state laws. Traditionally many persons were exempted from jury duty because of their jobs. The exemptions varied from state to state, but the most common exemptions were for lawyers, doctors, dentists, pharmacists, teachers and the clergy. In some states nurses, journalists, printers, railroad, telegraph, and telephone employees, government officials, firefighters, and police officers were also exempt. Generally, persons were exempt because the jobs they did were considered so important to society that they couldn't be released from them for jury duty.

However, these automatic exemptions and excuses are becoming less and less common. The American Bar Association's Standards Relating to Jury Use say that all automatic excuses and exemptions should be eliminated, and in 27 states they have been sharply cut back or completely done away with.

On occasion, the qualifications of all the potential jurors may be challenged, on the grounds that the jury pool—which is to represent the whole community—excludes certain groups. This is called a *challenge to the array* and generally is based on the allegation that court officials compiled the jury list in an illegal manner.

Once the jury list is assembled, juries of six to twelve persons are selected from this pool. The size of jury varies from state to state and depends to some extent on the type of case at trial. In civil cases, especially in courts of limited jurisdiction, the standard size in many jurisdictions is becoming six, which can be increased by stipulation of both parties. In misdemeanor cases there are sometimes fewer than twelve jurors, though in serious criminal cases twelve jurors are generally required. The old requirement that juries be unanimous is also changing. In misdemeanor and civil cases particularly, states are experimenting with permitting verdicts based on the concurrence of three-fourths or five-sixths of the jurors.

Alternate jurors are selected in some cases to take the place of jurors who may become disabled during the trial. Alternate jurors hear the evidence just as the other jurors do, but they do not participate in the deliberations unless they replace an original juror.

Jury selection begins with the court clerk's calling twelve people on the jury list and asking them to take a place in the jury box. The judge usually makes a brief statement explaining what kind of case is to be tried and inquiring whether there is any reason the potential jurors cannot serve. The judge or the lawyers then ask them questions ranging from their names, occupations, and residences to whether they have any knowledge of the case. This questioning of the potential jurors is known as *voir dire*.

If either lawyer believes there is information which suggests a juror is prejudiced about the case, he or she can ask that the juror be dismissed *for cause.* For example, a juror can be dismissed for cause if he or she is a close relative of one of the parties or one of the lawyers, or if he or she works for a company that is part of the lawsuit. A juror can only be dismissed for cause with the concurrence of the judge. Each lawyer may challenge an unlimited number of jurors for cause.

In addition to challenges for cause, each lawyer has a specific number of *peremptory challenges.* These challenges permit a lawyer to excuse a potential juror without stating a cause. In effect, they allow a lawyer to exercise a hunch, to dismiss a juror because of a belief that the juror will not be sympathetic. Peremptory challenges are limited to a certain number determined by the kind of lawsuit being tried.

When both parties have agreed upon a jury, the jurors are sworn in by the court clerk. Those not selected are excused from participating as jurors in the case.

Separating the Witnesses. In certain civil or criminal cases, either lawyer may advise the court that he or she wishes to sequester witnesses. This means that except for the plaintiff and the defendant, all witnesses will be kept out of the courtroom until they are called to testify. The idea behind this is that the witnesses' recollections will be more accurate if they haven't heard the other witnesses, so their testimony will be more accurate. (Sequestering the witnesses is sometimes referred to as *calling for the rule.*)

The witnesses are admonished by the judge not to discuss the case or their testimony with anyone except the lawyers. If neither side seeks to sequester the witnesses, the witnesses may remain in the courtroom until they testify.

Opening Statements. A trial begins with the opening statement of the party with the burden of proof.

In a criminal trial, the burden of proof rests with the state, which must prove beyond a reasonable doubt that the defendant is guilty.

In a civil trial, the plaintiff has the burden of proof, and generally must prove liability by a preponderance of the evidence (i.e., the greater weight of the evidence.) The degree of proof required in a civil case is far less stringent than in a criminal case.

The opening statement must be confined to facts that will be proved by the evidence, and it cannot be argumentative.

The defense lawyer follows with his or her opening statement. In some states, the defense may reserve its opening statement until the end of the plaintiff's or state's case. Either lawyer may choose not to present an opening statement.

Evidence. The heart of the case is the presentation of evidence. There are two types of evidence—direct and circumstantial—and they are offered in two forms—oral testimony of witnesses and physical exhibits, including documents. Direct evidence usually is that which speaks for itself: eyewitness accounts, a confession, a weapon or "instrumentality" of crime. Circumstantial evidence usually is that which suggests something by implication: the appearance of the scene of a crime, testimony that suggests a connection or link with a crime, physical evidence that suggests criminal activity.

It is very likely that both kinds of evidence are a part of most trials, with circumstantial evidence probably being used more often than direct.

Strict rules govern the kinds of evidence that may be admitted into a trial, and the presentation of evidence is governed by quite formal rules.

Lawyers for the plaintiff or the state begin the presentation of evidence by calling *witnesses*. The questions they ask of the witnesses are *direct examination*. (Direct examination is not restricted to direct evidence; it may elicit both direct and circumstantial evidence.) Witnesses may testify to matters of fact. They also may be called to identify documents, pictures or other items introduced into evidence.

Generally, witnesses cannot testify to *hearsay*. Hearsay is literally what the witness says he or she heard another person say. An example would be, "Bill said that John admitted shooting his wife." The witness is repeating a statement made by someone else, not what the witness actually saw or heard. In the words of *Black's Law Dictionary*, "hearsay does not derive its value solely from the credit of the witnesses, but rests mainly on the veracity and competency of other persons. The very nature of the evidence shows its weakness, and it is admitted only in specified cases from necessity."

An example of an exception under which hearsay evidence is admissible is a statement made spontaneously with the occurrence of a startling event. Such statements are admissible because experience and common sense have demonstrated that they are generally trustworthy because of their sudden, unpremeditated nature. Other exceptions are also recognized by federal and state rules of evidence.

Generally witnesses cannot state opinions or give conclusions unless they are experts or are especially qualified to do so. Witnesses qualified in a particular field as *expert witnesses* may give their opinion based on the facts in evidence and may give the reason for that opinion. Sometimes the facts in evidence are posed to experts in hypothetical questions. At other times experts are asked to state an opinion based on personal knowledge of the facts through their own examination or investigation.

Lawyers generally may not ask *leading questions* of their own witnesses. Leading questions are questions which suggest the answers desired, in effect prompting the witness. An example is, "Isn't it true that you saw John waiting across the street before his wife came home?"

Objections may be made by the opposing counsel to leading questions, questions that call for an opinion or conclusion by a witness, or questions that require an answer based on hearsay. There are many other reasons for objections.

Most courts require a specific reason be given for an objection. Usually, the judge will immediately either sustain or overrule the objection. If the objection is sustained, the lawyer must re-phrase the question in a proper form or ask another question. If the objection is overruled and the witness answers the question, the lawyer who raised the objection may appeal the judge's ruling after the trial is over.

Cross-Examination. When the lawyer for the plaintiff or the state has finished questioning a witness, the defense may then cross-examine the witness. Cross-examination is generally limited to questioning only on matters that were raised during direct examination. Leading questions may be asked during cross-examination, since the purpose of cross-examination is to test the credibility of statements made during direct examination. Another reason for allowing leading questions is that the witness is being questioned by the lawyer who did not originally call him or her, so it is likely that the witness will resist any suggestion which is not true.

On cross-examination, the attorney might try to question the witness's ability to identify or recollect or try to impeach the witness or the evidence. "Impeach" in this sense means to destroy or reduce the credibility of the witness or evidence. The attorney might do this by trying to show prejudice or bias in the witness, such as his or her relationship or friendship with one of the parties, or his or her interest in the outcome of the case. Witnesses may be asked if they have been convicted of a felony or a crime involving moral turpitude, since this is relevant to their credibility.

Opposing counsel may object to certain questions asked on cross-examination if the questions violate the state's laws on evidence or if they relate to matters not discussed during direct examination.

Re-Direct and Re-Cross Examination. After cross-examination, the lawyer who called the witness has the right to ask additional questions on re-direct examination. The re-direct examination covers new matters brought out in cross-examination and generally is an effort to rehabilitate a witness whose testimony on direct examination was weakened by cross-examination.

The opposing lawyer may then re-cross-examine, and re-re-direct may then follow, etc. until either the lawyers have finished or the judge calls an end to it.

Motion for Directed Verdict/Dismissal. At the conclusion of the plaintiff's or state's evidence, the lawyer will announce that the plaintiff or state rests. Then, when the jury leaves the courtroom, the defendant's lawyer in a civil case may make a motion for a directed verdict, arguing that his or her client's liability has not been proven by a preponderance of the evidence. In a criminal trial, the defendant's lawyer may ask for a motion to dismiss the charges, arguing that the government has failed to prove its case beyond a reasonable doubt. In effect, in both kinds of cases, the lawyer asks the judge to direct a verdict for the defendant. The judge will either grant or deny the motion. If it is granted, the case is over and the defendant wins. If the motion is denied, as it usually is, the defense is given the opportunity to present its evidence.

Presentation of Evidence by the Defense. The defense lawyer may choose to present no evidence in the belief that the plaintiff or state did not prove its case. Usually, however, the defense will call witnesses and present other evidence.

In a criminal case, the witnesses presented by the defense may or may not include the defendant. Because the Fifth Amendment to the U. S. Constitution protects against self-incrimination, the prosecution cannot require the defendant to take the stand and explain what happened.

The defense presents evidence in the same manner as the plaintiff or state, and the plaintiff or state in return has the right to cross-examine the defense's witnesses. Re-direct and re-cross examination also are permitted.

Rebuttal. At the conclusion of the defendant's case, the plaintiff or state can present rebuttal witnesses or evidence to refute evidence presented by the defendant. This may include only evidence not presented in the case initially, or a new witness who contradicts the defendant's witness.

After rebuttal, the defense then gets to present additional evidence.

Conferences During the Trial. Occasionally during the trial the lawyers will ask permission to approach the bench to speak to the judge, or the judge may call both lawyers to the bench. These are called *bench conferences* or *sidebars*. The court reporter will record everything said. During a bench conference the lawyers and the judge will speak quietly because the jurors might not understand the discussion or become prejudiced by what they hear.

Bench conferences deal with such questions as procedure, the conduct of the trial, juror misconduct, and mistrial motions.

Often a bench conference concerns whether certain evidence is admissible. Questions about the admissibility of evidence are for the judge to decide. If the judge cannot make a ruling quickly, the jury will be taken out of the courtroom and the judge will hear arguments.

Any time the jurors leave the courtroom, the judge will admonish them not to form an opinion or discuss the case with anyone.

Final Motions. After all the evidence has been presented and the jury has left the courtroom, either side may again move for a *directed verdict*. If the motion is granted the trial is over; if not, the presentation of evidence is complete and the case is ready to be submitted to the jury.

Closing Arguments. The lawyer for plaintiff or state often presents the first closing argument, or *summation*. The lawyer sums up and comments on the evidence in the most favorable light for his or her side.

Closing arguments include a discussion of the facts and properly drawn inferences. The judge usually indicates to the lawyers before closing arguments begin which instructions he or she intends to give the jury. It is proper for the lawyers in their closing arguments to comment on the jury instructions and to relate them to the evidence.

The lawyers cannot talk about issues outside the case or about evidence that was not presented.

After the plaintiff or state has made its case, the defense then presents its closing arguments. The defense lawyer usually answers statements made in the plaintiff's argument, points out defects in the plaintiff's case and sums up the facts favorable to his/her client.

Because the plaintiff or state has the burden of proof, its lawyer is then entitled to make the concluding argument to respond to the defendant and make a final appeal to the jury.

Occasionally the defense may choose not to make a closing statement. If so, the plaintiff or state loses the right to make a second argument.

Instructions to the Jury. After closing arguments, the judge instructs the jury about the relevant laws that should guide its deliberations. (In some jurisdictions, the court may instruct the jury at any time after the close of evidence. This sometimes occurs *before* closing arguments.) The judge reads the instructions to the jury. This is commonly referred to as the judge's *charge* to the jury.

In giving the instructions, the judge will state the issues in the case and define any terms or words that may not be familiar to the jurors. He or she will discuss the standard of proof that jurors should apply to the case—e.g., "beyond a reasonable doubt" in a criminal case, "preponderance of the evidence" in a civil case. The judge may read sections of applicable laws. The judge will advise the jury that it is the sole judge of the facts and of the credibility of witnesses. The judge will point out, however, that the instructions contain the interpretation of the relevant laws that govern the case, and that jurors are required to adhere to these laws in making their decision. In short, the jurors determine the facts and reach a verdict, within the guidelines of the law as interpreted by the judge.

Although the judge makes the final decisions about what jury instructions will be given, many states allow the lawyers to request that certain instructions be given. As noted above, the judge will usually tell the lawyers before closing arguments what instructions he or she intends to give the jury. This allows the lawyers to explain the instructions and to relate them to the facts of the case.

Mistrials. Mistrials are trials that are terminated and declared void before the jury returns a verdict or the judge renders his or her decision in a nonjury trial. Mistrials can occur for many reasons: for example, death of a juror or attorney, an improper drawing of the jury, a fundamental error prejudicial to the defendant that cannot be cured by appropriate instructions to the jury (such as the inclusion of highly improper remarks in the prosecutor's summation), or the jury's inability to reach a verdict because it is hopelessly deadlocked.

Either side may make a motion for a mistrial. The judge will either grant the motion and declare the trial a mistrial, or he or she will not grant the motion and the trial will go on.

A mistrial does not result in a judgment for any party, but merely indicates the failure of the trial. Because mistrials are not valid trials, the prohibition against double jeopardy (see below) does not apply to them. This means that criminal defendants whose trials result in mistrials can be tried again.

Jury Deliberations. After receiving the instructions, the jury retires to the jury room to begin deliberating. In most states the first order of business is to elect one of the jurors as the foreman or forewoman.

The bailiff sits outside the jury room to ensure that no one communicates with the jury during deliberations.

In some states, the jury may take the exhibits introduced into evidence and the judge's instructions to the jury room. Sometimes the jury will have a question about the evidence or the judge's instructions. If this happens, the jury will give a note to the bailiff to take to the judge. The judge may respond to the note, or may call the jury back into the courtroom for further instructions or to have portions of the transcript read to them.

Usually the court provides the jury with written forms of all possible verdicts, so that when a decision is reached, the jury has only to choose the proper verdict form.

In most instances, the verdict in a criminal case must be unanimous. In some states a less than unanimous decision is permitted in civil cases. All federal cases require a unanimous decision.

If the jury cannot come to a decision by the end of the day, the jurors may be *sequestered*, or housed in a hotel and secluded from all contact with other people, newspapers and news reports. In many cases, though, the jury will be allowed to go home at night, provided neither party objects.

If the jurors cannot agree on a verdict, a *hung jury* results, leading to a mistrial. The case is not decided, and it may be tried again at a later date before a new jury. However, if the plaintiff or state decides not to pursue the case further, it is over, and the defendant is free from civil liability or criminal punishment.

Decision. After reaching a decision, the jury notifies the bailiff, who notifies the judge. All of the participants reconvene in the courtroom and the decision is announced. The announcement may be made by either the foreman or the court clerk.

Possible verdicts in criminal cases are "guilty" or "not guilty." In a civil suit, the jury will find for the plaintiff or the defendant. If the jury finds for the plaintiff, it will also usually set out the amount of damages.

Sometimes verdicts other than these are possible. "Guilty but insane" is a possible verdict in some states. In some very complicated civil trials, when applying the law to the facts might be too difficult for a jury, the judge may simply ask the jury to decide one or more factual questions, and then the judge will apply the law to the facts as determined by the jury. This is called a "special verdict."

The lawyer for either party may ask that the jury be *polled*, although the request usually comes from the losing party. This means each juror will be asked if he or she agrees with the decision, as announced. The reason they are asked is to make sure that the verdict announced is the actual verdict of the jury. After the decision is read and accepted by the court, the jury is dismissed, and the trial is over.

Motions after Verdict. Motions permitted after a verdict is announced differ from state to state.

A *motion in arrest of judgment* questions the sufficiency of the indictment or information in a criminal case and asks that the judgment not be enforced.

A motion for *judgment notwithstanding the verdict* may be made after the jury's decision is announced but before a judgment is entered. This motion asks the judge to enter a judgment for the losing party despite the decision of the jury.

A *motion for a new trial* asks for a new trial to be granted, based on errors committed by the judge during the trial. In some states, the losing party must make a motion for a new trial before filing an appeal.

Judgment. The decision of the jury does not take effect until the judge enters a *judgment* on the decision.

In a civil suit, the judge usually has the authority to increase or decrease the amount of damages awarded by the jury, or to make some other modifications before entering judgment. In criminal cases, the judge generally has no authority to modify the verdict. He or she must accept it or reject it (e.g., by granting a motion for judgment notwithstanding the verdict).

If the defendant does not pay the damages awarded to the plaintiff in a civil case, the plaintiff may ask for an *execution* of the judgment. The clerk of the court in such a case will deliver the execution to the sheriff, commanding him to take and sell the property of the defendant and apply that money to the amount of the judgment.

Sentencing. If the defendant is convicted in a criminal case, the judge will set a date for sentencing. At that time, the judge may consider mitigating facts or other information developed in a pre-sentence investigation in determining the appropriate sentence.

The pre-sentence investigation may consider the defendant's prior criminal record, family situation, health, work record, and any other relevant factor, in an effort to help the judge find the most appropriate sentence.

In most states and in the federal courts, it is solely the judge's function to determine the sentence to be imposed, as long as the sentence falls within the possible punishment set forth in the statutes. Some states allow the jury to recommend a sentence. This often happens when the death penalty is a possible sentence. A number of states have sentencing guidelines to guide judges in determining appropriate sentences and to encourage uniformity.

APPEALS

Rights of Appeal. In a civil case, either party may appeal to a higher court. In a criminal case, only the defendant has a right to an appeal in most states. (Some states give the prosecution a limited right to appeal to determine certain points of law. Full appeals by the prosecution generally are not allowed, however, because of the prohibition in the U. S. Constitution against *double jeopardy*, or being tried twice for the same crime.)

Criminal defendants convicted in state courts also have a further appellate safeguard. They may file a writ of habeas corpus in the federal courts in an attempt to show that their federal constitutional rights were violated. The right of a federal review imposes the check of the federal judiciary on abuses that may occur in the state courts.

Appeals in either civil or criminal cases are usually made on the grounds of errors in trial procedure or errors in the judge's interpretation of the law. There are other grounds for appeal, but these are the most common.

The record on appeal consists of the papers filed in the trial court and the court reporter's transcript of the trial. The transcript must be certified by the trial judge as true and correct. In most states, only the relevant parts of the transcript—e.g., the ones relating to the points being appealed—are included in the appeal.

Appeal Procedure. The party appealing is called the *appellant*, or sometimes the *petitioner*. The other party is the *appellee* or the *respondent*.

The appeal is instituted with the filing of a *notice of appeal*. This filing marks the beginning of the time period within which the appellant must file a *brief*, a written argument containing that side's view of the facts and the legal arguments upon which the appellant relies in seeking a reversal of the trial court.

The appellee then has a specified time to file an answering brief. The appellant may then file a second brief answering the appellee's brief.

Many state and federal appeals courts generally make their decision on the basis of the briefs, without hearing oral arguments. (In the fiscal year ending June 30, 1986, 45.6% of the appellate decisions rendered on the merits of the controversy occurred after proceedings which did not include oral arguments.) Or the case may be set for *oral argument* before the appellate court. Sometimes the court will ask that the case be set for oral argument; at other times one of the parties will request oral argument. At oral argument, each side's attorney is given a relatively brief opportunity to argue the case to the court, and to answer questions posed by the judges. In the U.S. Supreme Court, for example, an hour is set for oral argument of most cases, which gives each side's lawyers about half an hour to make their oral argument and answer questions from the justices.

The job of the appellate court is to determine whether the law was followed during the trial. An appellate court generally will reverse a trial court only for an error of law.

Not every error of law, however, is cause for a reversal. Some are *harmless errors* that did not prejudice the rights of the parties to a fair trial. For example, in a criminal case a higher court may conclude that the judge who presided over the trial gave a legally improper instruction to the jury, but if the mistake were relatively minor and in the opinion of the appellate court had no bearing on the jury's finding, the appellate court may hold it to be a harmless error and let the decision stand. However, an error of law such as the admission of improper evidence may be determined to be harmful and therefore *reversible error.*

After a case is orally argued or otherwise presented for the judgment of the appellate court, the judges will meet in conference to discuss the case. Almost all appellate courts are required to issue written decisions. At the conference, one judge will be designated to write an opinion. The opinion may go through several drafts before a majority of the court agrees with it. Judges disagreeing with the *majority opinion* may issue a *dissenting opinion.* Judges agreeing with the result of a majority decision but disagreeing with the the majority's reasoning may file a *concurring opinion.*

Published appellate court decisions begin with a brief summary of the opinion. Then, the opening portion of the majority opinion usually states the facts of the case and the legal issues the court has been asked to decide. The middle portion of the opinion sets out the court's reasoning in reaching its decision and the previous appellate decisions that support that reasoning. The closing portion contains the decision and states what further action is to be taken in the case.

After the opinion is handed down and time for a rehearing has expired, or a rehearing has been denied, the appellate court will send its *mandate* to the trial court for further action. If the lower court's judgment is affirmed, the case ends, unless the losing party appeals to a higher court. If the judgment is reversed, the appellate court's mandate may order that a new trial be held, or that the trial court's judgment be modified or corrected. Appeals may also be dismissed (usually for reasons of jurisdiction) or sent back to a lower court (remanded) for reconsideration of the facts or for many other reasons.

An appeal in a civil case ordinarily does not prevent the enforcement of the trial court's judgment. The winning party in the trial court may order the judgment executed unless the appealing party files an *appeal* or *supersedeas bond.* The filing of this bond will prevent, or *stay,* further action on the judgment until the appeal is over by guaranteeing that the appealing party will pay or perform the judgment if it is not reversed on appeal.

COURTROOM DESIGN: ALTERNATIVE #2

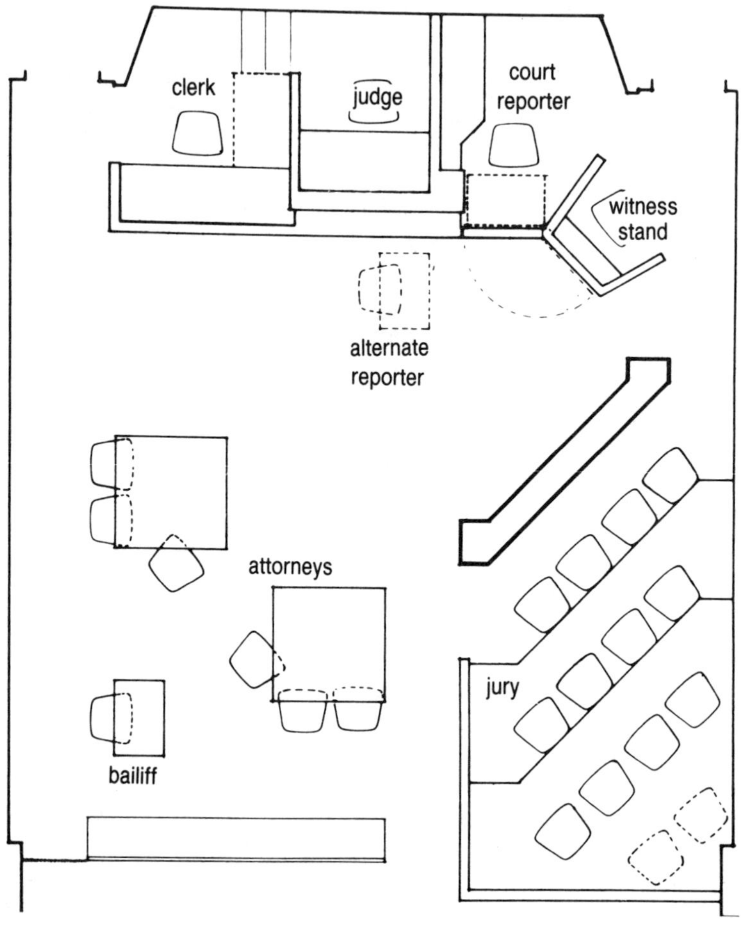

Visual and acoustic considerations are predominant in this courtroom design featuring a diagonally stepped jury arrangement and an elevated judge's bench.

Free Press/Fair Trial

Fundamental to our legal system is the guarantee of a fair trial by an impartial jury, based on evidence presented in open court. Also fundamental to the system of democratic self-government is the principle that the functions of government, including the courts, be conducted openly and in public view. At times, the U.S. Constitution's Sixth Amendment guarantee of a fair trial and the First Amendment right to a free press have come into conflict with each other.

Events in recent years have focused increased national attention on the issues involved in preserving both of these fundamental rights—fair trial and free press. Particularly during the last decade, there have been substantial developments leading to an accommodation of these complementary rights, resulting in greater access by the press and the public to witness legal proceedings and legal affairs.

One of the landmark cases in this area involved a sensational murder case. In 1954, Dr. Samuel H. Sheppard of Bay Village, Ohio, a suburb of Cleveland, was accused of murdering his wife. The case immediately attracted the attention of both the local and national media. Dozens of reporters from all over the country came to Cleveland, and the glare of publicity took the charges out of their normal context and disrupted the control of the court over the trial. In 1966, the U.S. Supreme Court ruled in the case of *Sheppard v. Maxwell* that Dr. Sheppard had been deprived of a fair trial by excessive publicity both in the pre-trial and trial stages. The Court held that "trial courts must take strong measures to ensure that the balance is never weighted against the accused."

Among the problems created by massive prejudicial publicity are difficulty in maintaining the presumption of the defendant's innocence, difficulty in empanelling an impartial jury, difficulty in confining the jury's deliberations to facts brought out in testimony at the trial, and difficulty in maintaining order and decorum in the courtroom.

In late 1975, a grisly murder in Nebraska raised a number of these considerations. The case, which took place in a town of under 1000 people, involved the murder of a six-person family and the rape of a ten-year-old girl. The judge presiding over the preliminary public hearing (held to determine that cause exists to hold an arrested person for trial) tried to forestall prejudicial publicity by barring the press from reporting on the proceedings of the hearing.

In the case of *Nebraska Press Association v. Stuart*, the U.S. Supreme Court ruled in 1976 that the need to forestall prejudicial publicity does not include barring the news media from publishing information gathered in open court.

During the 1980s the issue became not whether the press could report what it observed of court proceedings, but whether the press (and sometimes the public) could be barred entirely from certain proceedings.

When the cases ultimately reached the Supreme Court, the Court went on to recognize, and begin to define, a constitutional right of access to information about legal proceedings, primarily in the context of criminal cases. In these cases, the Supreme Court made clear that the public and press enjoy a qualified constitutional right to attend various kinds of legal proceedings.

In *Richmond Newspapers, Inc. v. Virginia*, a 1980 case, the Court ruled that excluding the public and press from a criminal trial in its entirety violates the First Amendment, unless the judge finds such a probability of prejudicial publicity that only this drastic measure will assure a fair trial. The judge must issue written findings justifying the move, and the hearing on whether the trial should be closed must be open to the public.

In the 1982 case of *Globe Newspaper Co. v. Superior Court*, the Court struck down as unconstitutional a law that imposed a wholesale exclusion of the public and press from trial testimony by minors who are complaining witnesses in sex crime cases. And in the 1984 decision in *Press Enterprise v. Superior Court*, the Supreme Court recognized that a First Amendment right of access to judicial proceedings was violated by an order sealing the transcript of *voir dire* (jury selection) proceedings in a death case. *Press-Enterprise II*, a later case, extended the presumption of openness to felony pre-trial hearings as conducted in California.

In deciding whether there is a right of public access to particular kinds of legal proceedings or records, the Supreme Court has looked to whether access would provide the public with information relevant to the discussion of governmental affairs and activity. This question in turn may encompass whether the kind of proceeding has been historically open to the public and, perhaps of more significance, whether opening the proceedings would contribute to the function of self-government and the democratic process.

In general, the Court has held that unless there is a very strong showing of harm to the judicial process, the public has a right to be present at proceedings that are normally open.

Even where there is a First Amendment right of public access to judicial proceedings or records, however, that right is necessarily qualified to accommodate the Sixth Amendment guarantee that litigants are entitled to a fair trial free of undue publicity. Therefore, an ordinarily public judicial proceeding may be closed where a trial court specifically finds that there are weighty and overriding reasons to do so in a particular case, and where there are no reasonable available alternatives to closure.

The delicate balancing of these rights of free press and fair trial continues to develop, especially in such areas as access to discovery in civil cases and to pre-trial depositions and discovery materials generally.

Also of continuing controversy has been the question of whether to ban television and still cameras in courtrooms. The issue here is the effect of these media on the orderly process of justice, as well as their effect on the defendant's right to a fair trial. For many years, cameras were banned in almost all courtrooms. This ban can be traced to the 1935 trial of the man accused of kidnapping Charles Lindbergh's baby, which attracted so much media attention that a circus atmosphere was created.

In the intervening years, new technology reduced the need for extra lights, obtrusive electrical cables, and other obvious manifestations of the media which might disrupt court proceedings. As a result, while there remains a ban on TV coverage inside federal courtrooms, except for certain ceremonial proceedings, the state supreme courts have taken the initiative to change this longstanding ban. These state initiatives, most of which began in the late 70s, and continue to the present, have been the result of urging by the broadcast media, which have persuaded judges that the presence of television and still cameras in courts need not interfere with the orderly process of justice or a defendant's right to a fair trial. By June of 1987, 42 states permitted cameras in the courtroom to varying degrees, and one state (Texas) permitted audio coverage only.

The effort to reach an accommodation of fair trial and free press rights will likely entail both additional adjudication and further cooperation between the bar and the media. These cooperative efforts to find a solution acceptable to all parties—including the press, the bar, the courts, and law enforcement agencies—have led to the creation of bench-bar-media committees in many communities. Some of these groups have drafted voluntary guidelines specifying types of information which, if published in advance of trial, are likely to be prejudicial to the defendant or otherwise raise serious public policy concerns.

In a similar vein, the American Bar Association in 1978 updated its Standards Relating to Fair Trial and Free Press after hearing news media views and concerns. The standards call for more access to judicial proceedings and fewer restrictions on press coverage of judicial proceedings in and around the courtroom. The standards suggest that the media be given standing in court to challenge trial judges' rulings restricting press coverage. Today, ABA committees and bench-bar-media committees in the states continue to address fair trial and free press rights and concerns.

While the courts will no doubt continue to be asked to adjudicate fair trial/free press issues, these issues are increasingly being resolved in a less confrontational atmosphere. This may be the result of increasing news media sensitivity to problems raised by publicizing potentially prejudicial information, including information on aspects of crimes, as well as greater awareness by attorneys and judges about the value of more accurate news coverage of the judicial system and the courts.

Further Resources / Readings

ON COURTS IN GENERAL

For information about a wide range of matters pertaining to criminal procedure, call the National Criminal Justice Reference Service, 800-638-8736 (Maryland residents call: 301-251-5139).

The Encyclopedia of the American Judicial System (New York: Scribner's, 1987) is a most useful resource for anyone seriously interested in American courts. This three-volume set was edited by Robert J. Janosik.

State and Federal Court Systems—A Guide (Cambridge, Mass: Ballinger, 1977), by Fannie Klein, is also of considerable use.

THE FEDERAL COURT SYSTEM

For specific information about the U.S. Supreme Court, contact the Public Information Officer, the Supreme Court of the United States, Washington, D.C. 20543. For information about other federal courts, contact the Public Information Officer, Administrative Office of United States Courts, Washington, D.C. 20544. The Information Service of the Federal Judicial Center (Dolley Madison House, Lafayette Square, 1520 H Street, N.W., Washington, D.C. 20005) is a particularly useful source of information about federal courts.

Several useful, brief handbooks on the federal court system are available from the Administrative Office of the U.S. Courts, at the address listed above. In only 23 pages, "The United States Courts: Their Jurisdiction and Work" provides a quick look at the differences between state and federal jurisdiction and the work of the various courts. "Glossary of Terms Used in the Federal Courts" includes a narrative introduction to some of the most common terms and procedures.

Preview of United States Supreme Court Cases is a unique resource for journalists, lawyers and others seeking up-to-date information on cases the Supreme Court is considering but has not yet decided. By providing an analysis of each case's issues, facts, background and significance, *Preview* helps readers better understand decisions when they are rendered. Available in yearly subscriptions from the American Bar Association's Public Education Division, 750 N. Lake Shore Drive, Chicago, Ill. 60611.

The Brethren (New York: Simon and Schuster, 1979), by Bob Woodward and Scott Armstrong, provides a behind-the-scenes look at the Supreme Court at work.

Equal Justice Under Law: The Supreme Court in American Life (Washington: Supreme Court Historical Society, 1982), by Mary Ann Harrell and Burnett Anderson, is a lively, crowded history of the Court and its achievements. Available from The Supreme Court Historical Society, 111 Second Street, N.E., Washington, D.C. 20002.

Gideon's Trumpet (New York: Random House, 1964), by Anthony Lewis, is a very readable look at the landmark Supreme Court case on the right to counsel.

Storm Center (New York: W. W. Norton & Company, 1986), by David O'Brien, looks at the Court, its operations, and the appointment of its justices from a political perspective.

The Supreme Court and Its Justices (Chicago: American Bar Association, 1987) includes articles from the *ABA Journal* on the internal operation of the Court, the appointment of justices, and lawyering before the Court. Available from Order Fulfillment 299-0013, American Bar Association, 750 N. Lake Shore Drive, Chicago, Ill. 60611.

STATE AND LOCAL COURTS

The public information office of the National Center for State Courts (300 Newport Avenue, Williamsburg, Va. 23187-8798) is able to provide data on state courts. Courts themselves are a natural, and generally useful, source of information. Many courts have handbooks for the general public explaining their procedures. They also often put out materials for jurors, witnesses, and others who become involved in the work of the courts. To find out more about the courts in your area, contact your state court administrator or the state supreme court (both located in the state capital).

Your local bar association or state bar association can also be a good source of information. Bar associations often provide guides to the courts, handbooks for jurors and witnesses, and other materials to explain the court system to the general public. Many bar associations also sponsor bar-bench-media conferences to improve communication between the press and the courts, and some have created materials specifically for journalists covering the courts in their area.

Explaining the Courts: Materials and Sources (Chicago: American Bar Association, 1983) is a bibliography covering a wide range of materials on the courts, including a number of materials explaining state and local courts. It is available from Order

Fulfillment 410-0001, American Bar Association, 750 N. Lake Shore Drive, Chicago, Ill. 60611.

Several books provide a helpful look at the judicial process. Seymour Wishman's *Anatomy of a Jury: The System on Trial* (New York: Times Books/Random House, 1986) and Peter N. Simon, *Anatomy of a Lawsuit* (Charlottesville, Va.: Michie Co., 1984) go through the steps in actual cases. Two other books, one that concentrates on the criminal process and the other on the civil process, are *How Can You Defend Those People?: The Making of a Criminal Lawyer* by James S. Kunen (New York: McGraw Hill, 1983) and *The Biography of a Legal Dispute: An Introduction to American Civil Procedure* by Marc A. Franklin (New York: Foundation Press, 1968). Finally, many public libraries contain state code books (books of state laws) and other useful references.

COVERING THE COURTS

A number of books touch on various aspects of reporting on law and the courts.

Reporter and the Law (New York: Hastings House, 1980), by Lyle Denniston, is probably the most comprehensive treatment of how the media can cover the many courts that exist in all jurisdictions.

News Making in the Trial Courts (New York: Longman, 1983), by Robert E. Drechfel, is a worthwhile book on the coverage of trials and the relationship between reporters and their court sources (judges and lawyers).

Free Press and Fair Trial: Values in Concert (Washington, D.C.: American Society of Newspaper Editors, American Newspaper Publishers Association Foundation, revised edition, 1987) is one of a number of books on how the law itself affects journalists' work. It looks at the interplay between the First and Sixth amendments.

Synopsis of the Law of Libel and the Right of Privacy (New York: Pharos Books, revised edition, 1984), by Bruce W. Sanford, and *Libel, Law and the Press: Myth and Reality* (New York: Free Press, 1987), by Randall P. Bezanson, Gilbert Cransbert and John Soloski, look at another legal dimension of the reporter's work.

THE ABA STANDARDS

The American Bar Association has established standards and guidelines in many areas of court procedure. Though not adopted in every jurisdiction, they serve to guide the work of state and federal courts.

A wide variety of ABA standards deal directly with the courts. See *Standards for Traffic Justice, Standards of Judicial Administration, Standards Relating to Appellate Courts, Standards Relating to Court Delay Reduction, Standards Relating to Court Organization, Standards Relating to Juror Use and Management, Standards Relating to Trial Courts.* All are avilable from Order Fulfillment, 750 N. Lake Shore Drive, Chicago, Ill. 60611.

The ABA Guidelines for the Evaluation of Judicial Performance deal with judicial competence. They are available from ABA Evaluation of Judicial Performance Project, 1800 M Street, South Lobby, 2nd Floor, Washington, D.C. 20036-5886, (202) 331-2267.

The ABA Standards on Juvenile Justice provide another useful source of information. The standards are available from Ballinger Publishing Company, 17

Dunster Street, Cambridge, Ma. 02138.

The ABA Criminal Justice Standards are also of considerable use. Available from Little, Brown & Co., 200 West Street, P.O. Box 9131, Waltham, Ma. 02254-9931

OTHER ASPECTS OF LAW AND THE COURTS

Court houses and courtrooms belong to the world of architecture as well as to the world of law. The most striking book on the subject is *Court House*, edited by Richard Pare and published in 1978 by the Horizon Press. It contains a number of photographs of courts, as well as essays on the architecture and history of courts.

The American Courthouse: Planning and Design for the Judicial Process is another excellent book on the architecture of courts. This joint publication of the American Bar Association and the American Institute of Architects is an interdisciplinary guide to the design of court facilities. It is the source of the courtroom design alternatives reprinted on pages 30, 56, 69, and 75. Available from Order Fulfillment, American Bar Association, 750 N. Lake Shore Drive, Chicago, IL 60611.

Many state and local courts have booklets explaining the role of jurors. For questions about juries generally, contact the Center for Jury Studies, 4001 North Ninth Street, Suite 218, Arlington, Va. 22203.

A number of publications provide information about alternative dispute resolution.

Alternative Dispute Resolution: An ADR Primer (Washington: American Bar Association, 1987) is a useful look at a number of alternatives. It is available from the ABA's Standing Committee on Dispute Resolution, American Bar Association, 1800 M Street, N.W., Washington, D.C. 20036.

Mediation: A Comprehensive Guide to Resolving Conflict Without Litigation (San Francisco, Ca.: Jossey-Bass, 1984), by Jay Folberg and Alison Taylor, and *Mediation Process: Practical Strategies for Resolving Conflicts* (San Francisco, Ca.: Jossey-Bass, 1986), by Christopher W. Moore, look at a popular form of ADR.

Dispute Resolution in America: Processes in Evolution (1984), by S.B. Goldberg, E.D. Green and F.E.A. Sander, is available from the National Institute for Dispute Resolution, 1901 L Street, N.W., Washington, D.C. 20036.

Everybody's Guide to Small Courts (Berkeley, Ca.: Nolo Press, rev. ed. 1987), by Ralph Warner, is one of several helpful books on small claims courts.

Glossary of Legal Terms

This glossary defines a number of terms in common legal use which are not generally understood by lay people. It does not include the obscure and the obvious, defining neither arcane legal procedures which are little used nor terms which are generally well understood by the public. A number of books on the law for non-lawyers contain glossaries. Check your library or bookstore. For reporters covering the courts, a more complete glossary can be found in Lyle Denniston's *The Reporter and the Law* (New York: Hastings House, 1980). Definitions of several terms in this glossary have been adapted from *Barron's Dictionary of Legal Terms* (New York: Barron's Educational Series, 1983), a useful simplified guide to the language of the law. (A fuller version of this book, *Barron's Law Dictionary*, contains an additional 1,000 entries.) Several definitions have also been adapted from the massive *Black's Law Dictionary* (West Publishing Company). While intended for lawyers, this dictionary defines a very wide range of terms and can serve as a useful resource.

A

abstract of title A chronological summary of all official records and recorded documents affecting the title to a parcel of real property.

accomplice A person who knowingly and voluntarily unites with the principal offender in a criminal act through aiding, abetting, advising, or encouraging the offender.

acquittal A verdict after a trial that a defendant in a criminal case has not been proven guilty beyond a reasonable doubt of the crime charged.

action Case, cause, suit or controversy disputed or contested before a court of justice.

actus reus Proof that a criminal act has occurred.

additur An increase by a judge in the amount of damages awarded by a jury.

adjudication Giving or pronouncing a

judgment or decree; also the judgment given.

ad litem A Latin term meaning for the purposes of the lawsuit. For example, a guardian "ad litem" is appointed to prosecute or defend a suit on behalf of an incapacitated person.

admissible Evidence which can be legally and properly introduced in a civil or criminal trial.

adversary proceeding One having opposing parties; contested (differs from **ex parte** proceeding).

adversary system The trial methods used in the U.S. and some other countries, based on the belief that truth can best be determined by giving opposing parties full opportunity to present and establish their evidence, and to test by cross-examination the evidence presented by their adversaries, under established rules of procedure before an impartial judge and/or jury.

affiant A person who makes and signs an affidavit.

affidavit A written statement of fact given voluntarily and under oath. For example, in criminal crime cases, affidavits are often used by police officers seeking to convince courts to grant a warrant to make an arrest or a search. In civil cases, affidavits of witnesses are often used to support motions for summary judgment.

affirmed In the practice of appellate courts, the word means that the decree or order at issue is declared valid and will stand as rendered in the lower court.

affirmative defense Without denying the charge, defendant raises extenuating or mitigating circumstances such as insanity, self-defense, or entrapment to avoid civil or criminal responsibility.

allegation The statement in a pleading of what a party expects to prove. For example, an indictment contains allegations of crime against the defendant.

alternative dispute resolution Settling a dispute without a full, formal trial. Methods include **mediation, conciliation, arbitration, settlement,** among others.

amicus curiae A friend of the court; one not a party to a case who volunteers to offer information on a point of law or some other aspect of case to assist the court in deciding a matter before it.

answer The defendant's response to the plaintiff's allegations as stated in a complaint. An item-by-item, paragraph-by-paragraph response to points made in a complaint; part of the pleadings.

appeal A request by the losing party in a lawsuit that the judgment be reviewed by a higher court.

appearance Coming into court; the formal act by which a defendant submits to the jurisdiction of a court.

appellant The party who initiates an appeal. Sometimes called a **petitioner.**

appellate court A court having jurisdiction to hear appeals and review a trial court's procedure.

appellee The party against whom an appeal is taken. Sometimes called a **respondent.**

arbitration A form of **alternative dispute resolution,** in which the parties bring their dispute to a neutral third party and agree to abide by his or her decision. In arbitration there is a hearing at which both parties have an opportunity to be heard. Decisions usually can't be appealed.

arraignment In a criminal case, the proceeding in which an accused person is brought before a judge to hear the charges filed against him or her and to enter a plea of guilty or not guilty. Sometimes called **preliminary hearing** or **initial appearance.**

arrest To take into custody by legal authority.

assault Threat to inflict injury with an apparent ability to do so. Also, any intentional display of force which would give the victim reason to fear or expect immediate bodily harm.

at issue The contested points in a lawsuit are said to be "at issue."

attachment A proceeding in which a creditor secures rights to real or personal property and holds it pending the outcome of a lawsuit.

attorney-at-law An advocate, counsel, or official agent employed in preparing, managing, and trying cases in the courts. An officer in a court of justice, who is employed by a party in a cause to manage it for him.

attorney-in-fact A private attorney authorized by another to act in his place and stead, either for some particular purpose, as to do a particular act, or for the transaction of business in general, not of legal character. This authority is conferred by an instrument in writing, called a "letter of attorney," or more commonly a "power of attorney."

attorney of record The principal attorney in a lawsuit who signs all formal documents relating to the suit.

B

bail Money or other security (such as a **bail bond**) given to secure a person's release from custody, which is at risk should he or she subsequently fail to appear before the court. **Bail** and **bond** are often used interchangeably.

bail bond (often referred to simply as **bond**) The obligation, signed by the accused to secure his or her presence at trial, which he or she may lose by not properly appearing for trial.

bailiff A court attendant who keeps order in the courtroom and has custody of the jury.

bar Historically, the partition separating the general public from the space occupied by the judges, lawyers and other participants in a trial. More commonly, the term means the whole body of lawyers. The "case at bar" is the case currently being considered.

bar examination A state examination taken by prospective lawyers in order to be admitted to practice law.

battery A beating, or wrongful physical violence. The actual threat to use force is an **assault**; the use of it is a battery, which usually includes an assault.

bench The seat occupied by the judge; more broadly, the court itself.

bench warrant An order issued by a judge for the arrest of a person.

best evidence Primary evidence; the best evidence available; evidence short of this is "secondary"; i.e., an original letter is the "best evidence," a photocopy is "secondary evidence."

beyond a reasonable doubt The standard in a criminal case requiring that the jury be satisfied to a moral certainty that every element of a crime has been proven by the prosecution. This standard of proof does not require that the state establish absolute certainty by eliminating all doubt, but it does require that the evidence be so conclusive that all reasonable doubts are removed from the mind of the ordinary person.

bill of particulars A statement of the details of the charge made against the defendant.

bind over To hold a person for trial on bond (**bail**) or in jail. If the judicial official conducting a preliminary hearing finds probable cause to believe the accused committed a crime, he or she will "bind over" the accused, normally by setting bail for his or her appearance at trial.

booking The process of photographing, fingerprinting, and recording identifying data of a suspect following arrest.

breach of contract A legally inexcusable failure to perform a contractual obligation.

brief A written statement prepared by one side in a lawsuit to explain to the court its view of the facts of a case and the applicable law.

burden of proof In the law of evidence, the necessity or duty of affirmatively proving a fact or facts in dispute on an issue raised between the parties in a lawsuit. The responsibility of proving a point—the burden of proof—is not the same as the standard of proof. "Burden of proof" deals with which side must establish a point or points; "standard of proof" indicates the degree to which the point must be proven. For example, in a civil case the burden of proof rests with the plaintiff, who must establish his or her case by such standards of proof as "a preponderance of evidence" or "clear and convincing evidence."

C

capital crime A crime punishable by death.

caption The heading on a legal document listing the parties, the court, the case number and related information.

case law Law based on previous decisions of appellate courts, particularly the Supreme Court.

cause A lawsuit, litigation, or action. Any question, civil or criminal, litigated or contested before a court of justice.

cause of action The facts that give rise to a lawsuit.

caveat A warning; a note of caution.

certiorari A means of getting an appellate court to review a lower court's decision. The loser of a case will often ask the appellate court to issue a writ of certiorari, which orders the lower court to convey the record of the case to the appellate court and to certify it as accurate and complete. If an appellate court grants a writ of certiorari, it agrees to take the appeal. This is often referred to as "granting cert."

challenge An objection, such as when an attorney objects at a **voir dire** hearing to the seating of a particular person on a jury, civil or criminal; may be **challenge for cause**

or **peremptory challenge.**

challenge for cause Objection to the seating of a particular juror for a stated reason (usually bias or prejudice for or against one of the parties in the lawsuit); the judge has discretion to deny the challenge (differs from **peremptory challenge**).

chambers A judge's private office. A hearing in chambers takes place in the judge's office outside of the presence of the jury and the public.

change of venue Moving a lawsuit to another place for trial, often because pretrial publicity makes it difficult to empanel an impartial jury.

charge to the jury The judge's instruction to the jury concerning the law which applies to the facts of the case.

circumstantial evidence Evidence which merely suggests something by implication. For example, physical evidence, such as fingerprints, from which an inference can be drawn. Circumstantial evidence is indirect, as opposed to eyewitness testimony, which is direct.

citation A reference to a source of legal authority; also, a direction to appear in court, as when a defendant is cited into court rather than arrested.

civil actions Non-criminal cases in which one private individual or business sues another for redress of private or civil rights.

civil procedure Process by which a civil case is tried and appealed, including the preparations for trial, the rules of evidence and trial conduct, and the procedure for pursuing appeals.

class action A lawsuit brought by one or more persons on behalf of a larger group.

clear and convincing evidence Standard of proof commonly used in civil lawsuits and in regulatory agency cases. It governs the amount of proof that must be offered in order for the plaintiff to prevail.

clemency (also called **executive clemency**) Act of grace or mercy by the president or governor to ease the consequences of a criminal act, accusation or conviction; may take the form of **commutation** or **pardon**.

codicil An addition to a will.

commit To send a person to prison, asylum or reformatory pursuant to a court order of **mittimus.**

common law Law arising from tradition and judicial decisions, rather than from laws passed by the legislature. The common law originated in England and has been followed as the law in most American jurisdictions. It is also called **case law.**

commutation The reduction of a sentence, as from death to life imprisonment.

comparative negligence A legal doctrine by which acts of the opposing parties are compared to determine the liability of each to the other, making each liable only for his/her percentage of fault. See also **contributory negligence.**

complaint The legal document that usually begins a civil lawsuit. It states the facts and identifies the action the court is asked to take.

complainant The party who complains or sues; one who applies to the court for legal redress, also called the **plaintiff.**

concurrent sentence Sentences for more than one violation which are to be served at the same time rather than one after the other. Three five-year terms served concurrently add up to no more than five years imprisonment; three five year terms served consecutively impose a 15-year sentence. See also **cumulative sentence.**

concurring opinion An appellate court opinion by one or more judges that agrees with part but not all of the majority opinion in the case.

condemnation The legal process by which the government invokes its powers of **eminent domain** and takes privately owned real estate for public use, paying the owners just compensation.

consecutive sentences Successive sentences, one beginning at the expiration of another, imposed against a person convicted of two or more violations.

conservatorship Legal right given to a person to manage the property and financial affairs of a person deemed incapable of doing that for him or herself. (See also **guardianship**. Conservators have somewhat less responsibility than guardians).

contempt of court Willful disobedience of a judge's command or of an official court order.

continuance Postponement of a legal proceeding to a later date.

contract A legally enforceable agreement between two or more competent parties made either orally or in writing.

contributory negligence A legal doctrine that says that if the plaintiff in a civil action for negligence also was negligent, he or she cannot recover damages from the defendant for the defendant's negligence. Most jurisdictions have abandoned the doctrine

COURTROOM DESIGN: ALTERNATIVE #3

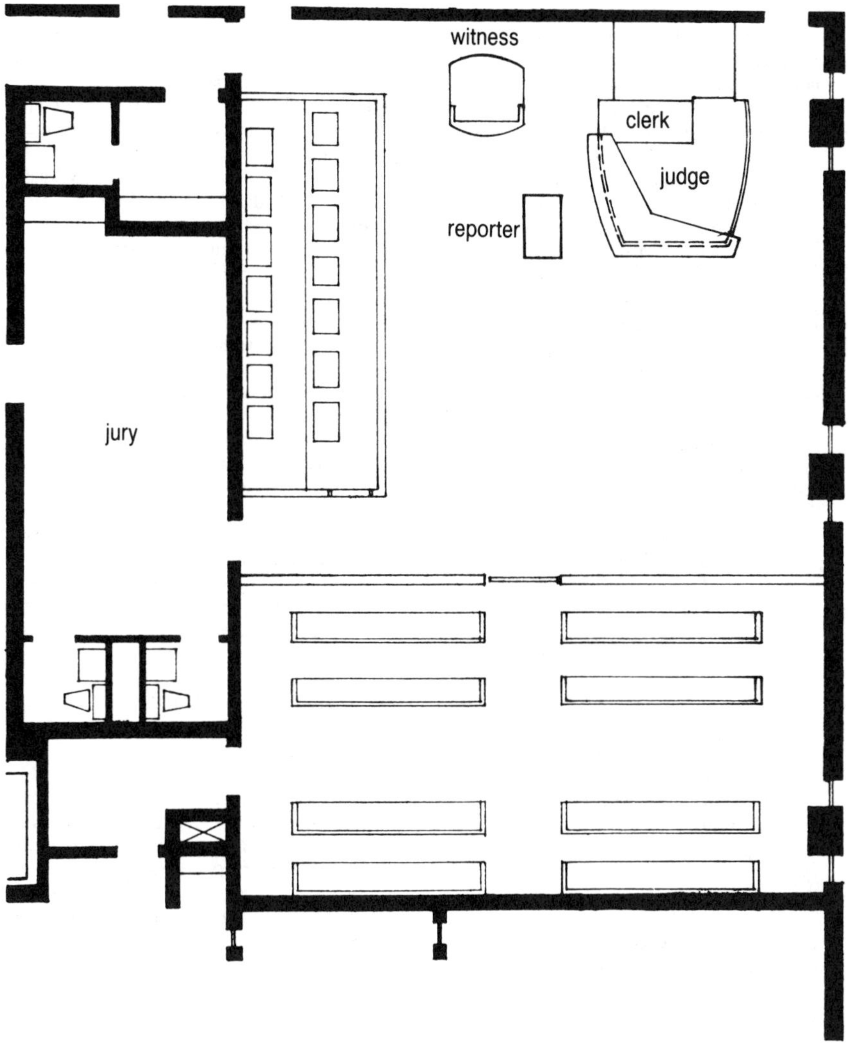

In this design, the jury room is right behind the jury box and the judge's bench is a unique boomerang shape with a built-in clerk's desk. Both the judge and jury have an excellent view of the witness.

of contributory negligence in favor of **comparative negligence**.

conviction A judgment of guilt against a criminal defendant.

copyright The right to literary property, giving authors, composers and other creators the sole right to reproduce and distribute their work for a limited period of time.

corpus delicti Body of the crime. The objective proof that a crime has been committed. Sometimes refers to the body of the victim of a homicide, or the charred shell of a burned house, but the term has a broader meaning. For the state to introduce a confession or convict the accused it must prove a corpus delicti, i.e., the occurrence of specific injury or loss and a criminal act as the source of the loss.

corroborating evidence Supplementary evidence that tends to strengthen or confirm the initial evidence.

counterclaim A claim made by the defendant in a civil lawsuit against the plaintiff—in essence, a counter lawsuit within a lawsuit.

court costs The expenses of prosecuting or defending a lawsuit other than attorney's fees. An amount of money may be awarded to the successful party (and recoverable from the losing party) as reimbursement for court costs.

cross-claim A claim by co-defendants or co-plaintiffs against each other and not against persons on the opposite side of the lawsuit.

cross-examination The questioning of a witness produced by the other side.

cumulative sentence Sentences for two or more crimes to run successively rather than concurrently.

D

damages Money awarded by a court to a person injured by the unlawful act or negligence of another person.

de novo Anew. A "trial de novo" is a new trial of a case.

decision The judgment reached or given by a court of law.

declaratory judgment A judgment which, without the need for enforcement, declares the rights of the parties or an interpretation of the law. For example, a court may be asked to issue a declaratory judgment on the constitutionality of a statute.

decree An order of the court. A final decree is one which fully and finally disposes of the litigation; an **interlocutory** decree is a preliminary order that often disposes of only part of a lawsuit.

default A failure to respond to a lawsuit within the specified time. When a defendant does not respond in a timely fashion or does not appear at the trial, a "default judgment" is entered against him or her.

defendant In a civil case, the person being sued. In a criminal case, the person charged with a crime.

demurrer A motion to dismiss a civil case because of the legal insufficiency of a complaint.

deposition The testimony of a witness taken under oath in preparation for a trial.

direct evidence Proof of facts by witnesses who saw acts done or heard words spoken, as distinguished from **circumstantial**, or indirect, evidence.

direct examination The first questioning of witnesses by the party on whose behalf they are called.

directed verdict An instruction by the judge to the jury to return a specific verdict.

disbarment Form of discipline of a lawyer resulting in the loss (often permanently) of his or her right to practice law (differs from censure and from suspension).

discovery The pre-trial process by which one party discovers the evidence that will be relied upon at trial by the opposing party.

dismissal The termination of a lawsuit. A "dismissal without prejudice" permits the suit to be filed again at a later time. In contrast, a "dismissal with prejudice" prevents the lawsuit from being filed later.

dissent An appellate court opinion setting forth the minority view and outlining the disagreement of one or more judges with the decision of the majority.

diversion The process of removing some minor criminal, traffic, or juvenile cases from the full judicial process, on the condition that the accused undergo some sort of rehabilitation or make restitution for damages. Diversion may take place before the trial or its equivalent, as when a juvenile accused of a crime may consent to probation without an admission of guilt. If he or she completes probation successfully—e.g., takes a course, makes amends for the crime—then the entire matter may be expunged from the record.

docket A list of cases to be heard by a court.

domicile The place where a person has his

permanent, legal home. A person may have several residences, but only one domicile.

double jeopardy Putting a person on trial more than once for the same crime; forbidden by the Fifth Amendment to the U.S. Constitution.

due process of law The right of all persons to receive the guarantees and safeguards of the law and the judicial process. Includes such constitutional requirements as adequate notice, assistance of counsel, and the rights to remain silent, to a speedy and public trial, to an impartial jury, and to confront and secure witnesses.

E

elements of a crime Specific factors that define a crime, every element of which the prosecution must prove beyond a reasonable doubt in order to obtain a conviction. The elements that must be proven are (1) that a crime has actually occurred, (2) that the accused intended the crime to happen, and (3) a timely relationship between the first two factors. See also **actus rea** and **mens rea**.

eminent domain The power of the government to take private property for public use through **condemnation.**

en banc All of the judges of a court sitting together. Appellate courts can consist of a dozen or more judges, but often they hear cases in panels of three judges. If a case is heard or re-heard by the full court, it is heard en banc.

enjoin To require a person, through the issuance of an injunction, to perform or to abstain from some specific act.

entrapment A defense to criminal charges alleging that agents of the government induced a person to commit a crime he or she otherwise would not have committed.

equal protection of the law The guarantee in the Fourteenth Amendment to the U.S. Constitution that all persons be treated equally by the law. Court decisions have established that this guarantee requires that courts be open to all persons on the same conditions, with like rules of evidence and modes of procedure; that persons be subject to no restrictions in the acquisition of property, the enjoyment of personal liberty, and the pursuit of happiness, which do not generally affect others; that persons are liable to no other or greater burdens than such are laid upon others; and that no different or greater punishment is enforced against them for a violation of the laws.

equity Generally, justice or fairness. Historically, equity refers to a separate body of law developed in England in reaction to the inability of the common-law courts, in their strict adherence to rigid writs and forms of action, to consider or provide a remedy for every injury. The king therefore established the court of chancery, to do justice between parties in cases where the common law would give inadequate redress. The principle of this jurisprudence is that equity will find a way to achieve a lawful result when legal procedure is inadequate. Equity and law courts are now merged in most jurisdictions, though equity jurisprudence and equitable doctrines are still independently viable.

escrow Money or a written instrument such as a deed which, by agreement between two parties, is held by a neutral third party ("held in escrow") until all conditions of the agreement are met.

estate A person's property and possessions.

et al. And others.

ex parte On behalf of only one party, without notice to any other party. For example, a request for a search warrant is an ex parte proceeding, since the person subject to the search is not notified of the proceeding and is not present during the hearing.

ex parte proceeding One in which only one side is represented (differs from **adversary system** or proceeding).

ex post facto After the fact. The Constitution prohibits the enactment of ex post facto laws, i.e., laws that permit conviction and punishment for a lawful act performed before the law was changed and the act made illegal.

exceptions Declarations by either side in a civil or criminal case reserving the right to appeal a judge's ruling upon a motion; also, in regulatory cases, objections by either side to points made by the other side or to rulings by the agency or one of its hearing officers.

exclusionary rule The rule preventing illegally obtained evidence to be used in any trial.

execute (a judgment or decree) To put the final judgment of the court into effect.

exhibit A document or other article introduced as evidence during a trial or hearing.

expungement Official and formal erasure

of a record or partial contents of a record.

extradition The process by which one state surrenders to another state a person accused or convicted of a crime in the other state.

F

felony A crime of a graver nature than a **misdemeanor**, usually punishable by imprisonment in a penitentiary for more than a year and/or substantial fines.

fiduciary A person having a legal relationship of trust and confidence to another and having a duty to act primarily for the other's benefit, e.g., a guardian, trustee, or executor.

finding Formal conclusion by a judge or regulatory agency on issues of fact; also, a conclusion by a jury regarding a fact.

first appearance The initial appearance of an arrested person before a judge to determine whether or not there is probable cause for his/her arrest. Generally the person comes before a judge within hours of arrest.

fraud Intentional deception to deprive another person of property or to injure that person in some other way.

G

garnishment A legal proceeding in which a debtor's money, in the possession of another (called the garnishee), is applied to the debts of the debtor, such as when one garnishes a debtor's wages.

good time A reduction in sentenced time in prison as a reward for good behavior; usually one-third to one-half off the maximum sentence.

grand jury A group of citizens, usually numbering twenty-three, who are assembled in secret to hear or investigate allegations of criminal behavior. A grand jury has authority to conduct criminal investigations and to charge a crime by **indictment**; also may have power to issue a report, or **presentment**, without charging a crime.

guardianship Legal right given to a person to be responsible for the food, housing, health care, and other necessities of a person deemed incapable of providing these necessities for himself or herself. A guardian may also be given responsibility for the person's financial affairs, and thus perform additionally as a conservator. (See also **conservatorship**).

guardian ad litem A person appointed by a court to look after the interests of a minor or an incapacitated person whose property or rights are involved in litigation.

H

habeas corpus A writ which commands that a person be brought before a judge. Most commonly, a writ of habeas corpus is a legal document that forces law enforcement authorities to produce a prisoner they are holding and to legally justify his or her detention.

harmless error An error committed during a trial which was corrected or was not serious enough to affect the outcome of a trial and therefore was not sufficiently harmful (prejudicial) to be reversed on appeal.

hearsay Evidence that is not within the personal knowledge of the witness but was relayed to the witness by a third party. Hearsay evidence generally is not admissible in court, although there are many exceptions under which it can be admitted.

hostile witness A witness whose testimony is not favorable to the party who calls him or her as a witness. A hostile witness may be asked leading questions and may be cross-examined by the party who calls him or her to the stand.

hung jury A jury that cannot reach a verdict.

I

immunity Grant by the court, in which someone will not face prosecution in return for providing criminal evidence (differs from **sovereign immunity**).

impeachment of a witness An attack on the credibility (believability) of a witness, through evidence introduced for that purpose.

in camera In chambers, or in private. A hearing in camera takes place in the judge's office outside of the presence of the jury and the public.

inadmissible That which under the rules of evidence cannot be admitted or received as evidence.

indeterminate sentence A sentence of imprisonment to a specified minimum and maximum period of time, specifically authorized by statute, subject to termination by a parole board or other authorized agency after the prisoner has served the minimum term.

indictment An accusation by a grand jury charging a person with a crime.

information Accusatory document, filed by the prosecutor, detailing the charges against the defendant. Used in states that do not have grand juries, it serves to bring a defendant to trial.

infraction A violation of law not punishable by imprisonment. Minor traffic offenses are generally considered infractions.

injunction A preventive measure by which a court orders a party to refrain from doing a particular act. A **preliminary injunction** is granted provisionally, until a full hearing can be held to determine if it should be made permanent.

instructions (also called **charge**) Judge's directions to the jury regarding the law in the case and its authority to determine the facts and to draw inferences from the facts in order to reach a verdict.

integrated bar Organized state bar association to which every lawyer in a state must belong in order to be permitted to practice in that state.

interlocutory Provisional; not final. An interlocutory order or an interlocutory appeal concerns only a part of the issues raised in a lawsuit.

interrogatories Written questions asked by one party of an adverse party for which written answers must be provided. (See also **depositions**).

intervention An action by which a third person who may be affected by a lawsuit is permitted to become a party to the suit. Differs from process by which one becomes an **amicus curiae**.

intestate One who dies without leaving a will.

issue (1) The disputed point or question to which the parties to a case have narrowed their disagreement; a single material point which is affirmed by one side and denied by the other. When the plaintiff and the defendant have arrived at some point which one affirms and the other denies, they are said to be "at issue." When the defendant has filed an answer denying all or part of the allegations of the complaint, the "issue has been joined" and the case is ready to be set for trial. (2) To send out officially (to issue an order).

J

joint and several liability A legal doctrine which makes each of the parties responsible for an injury liable for all of the damages awarded in a lawsuit if the other parties cannot pay.

judgment The final disposition of a lawsuit. **Default judgment** is a judgment rendered because of the defendant's failure to answer or appear. **Summary judgment** is judgment given on the basis of pleadings, affidavits, and exhibits presented for the record without any need for a trial. It is used when there is no dispute as to the facts of the case and one party is entitled to judgment as a matter of law. **Consent judgment** occurs when the provisions and terms of the judgment are agreed on by the parties and submitted to the court for its sanction and approval. A **judgment n.o.v.** is literally a judgment non obstante verdicto, which translates as **judgment notwithstanding the verdict**; it is a judge's decision to decide a case contrary to the verdict of the jury. It may be made in a civil or criminal case.

judicial review Authority of a court to review the official actions of other branches of government; also, authority to declare unconstitutional the actions of other branches.

jurisdiction The nature and scope of a court's authority to hear and/or decide a case. Also, the territory from which a court is authorized to hear cases.

jury A certain number of persons selected according to law and sworn to inquire into matters of fact and declare the truth about matters laid before them. A **grand jury** is traditionally composed of 23 people who decide whether the facts of a criminal case are sufficient to issue an indictment charging a person with a crime. A **petit jury** is an ordinary or trial jury, composed of six to twelve persons, which hears either civil or criminal cases.

jury commissioner The court officer responsible for choosing the panel of persons to serve as potential jurors for a particular court term.

justiciable Issues and claims properly examined in court.

L

larceny Obtaining property by fraud or deceit.

leading question A question which suggests the answer desired of the witness. A party generally may not ask one's own witness leading questions; leading questions may be asked only of hostile witnesses and on cross-examination.

legal aid Professional legal services available usually to persons or organizations unable to afford such services.

legislative history Background of action by a legislature, including testimony before committees, written reports and debates on the legislation.

leniency Recommendation by the prosecutor to the judge regarding the sentence that may be imposed in a criminal case.

liable Legally responsible for.

libel Published words or pictures that falsely and maliciously defame a person. Libel is published; **slander** is spoken.

lien A legal claim against another person's property as security for a debt. A lien does not convey ownership of the property, but gives the lienholder a right to have his or her debt satisfied out of the proceeds of the property if the debt is not otherwise paid.

limine A motion requesting that the court exclude certain evidence that might prejudice the jury.

litigant A party to a lawsuit.

litigation A case, controversy, or lawsuit.

M

magistrate Judicial officer exercising some of the functions of a judge; also, refers in a general way to a judge, as in the phrase "neutral magistrate."

mala in se "Evil in itself"—behavior that is universally regarded as criminal, such as murder.

mala prohibita - "Wrong because prohibited"—behavior that is criminal only because a society defines it as such. An example is the manufacture of alcoholic beverages during Prohibition.

mandamus A writ issued by a court ordering a public official to perform an act.

manslaughter The unlawful killing of another without intent to kill; either voluntary—upon a sudden impulse, i.e., a quarrel erupts into a fist-fight in which one of the participants is killed; or involuntary—during the commission of an unlawful act not ordinarily expected to result in great bodily harm, or during the commission of a lawful act without proper caution, i.e., driving an automobile at excessive speed resulting in a fatal collision. (See also **murder**.)

mediation A form of **alternative dispute resolution**, in which the parties bring their dispute to a neutral third party, who helps them agree on a settlement.

memorialized In writing.

mens rea The "guilty mind" necessary to establish criminal responsibility.

"Miranda warning" Requirement that police tell a suspect in their custody of his/her constitutional rights before they question him/her, so named as a result of the *Miranda v. Arizona* ruling establishing such requirements.

misdemeanor Criminal offenses considered less serious than **felonies**. Misdemeanors generally are punishable by a fine or a limited local jail term, but not by imprisonment in a state penitentiary.

mittimus The name of a precept in writing, issuing from a court and directing the sheriff or other officer to convey a person to prison, and directing the jailer to receive and safely keep the person until he or she shall be delivered by due course of law.

mistrial A trial which is terminated before a verdict is reached, either because of some extraordinary circumstance, because of fundamental error prejudicial to the defendant (such as an improper drawing of jurors), or because of a **hung jury**.

moot A moot case or a moot point is one not subject to a judicial determination because it involves an abstract question or a pretended controversy which has not yet actually arisen or has already passed. Mootness usually refers to a court's refusal to consider a case because the issue involved has been resolved prior to the court's decision, leaving nothing which would be affected by the court's decision.

motion An application for a rule or order, made to a court or judge.

murder The unlawful killing of a human being with malice aforethought. Murder in the first degree is characterized by premeditation; murder in the second degree is characterized by a sudden and instantaneous intent to kill or to cause injury

COURTROOM DESIGN: ALTERNATIVE #4

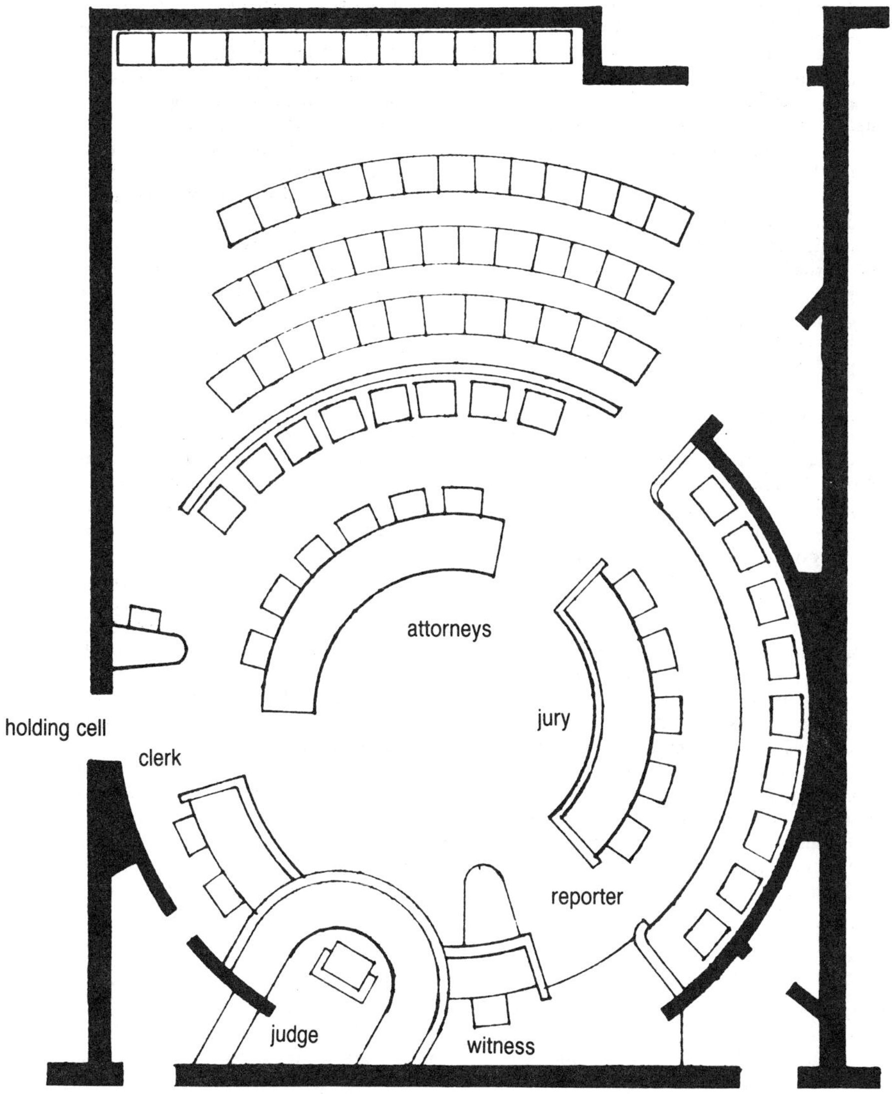

This courtroom is part of the Hall of Justice in Marin County, California. The building was designed by Frank Lloyd Wright.

without caring whether the injury kills or not. (See also **manslaughter**).

N

negligence Failure to exercise that degree of care which a reasonable man would exercise under the same circumstances. See also **comparative negligence** and **contributory negligence**.

neighborhood justice center In many areas of the country, neighborhood justice centers help parties resolve their disputes outside the traditional justice system, through **arbitration, mediation**, or some other form of **alternative dispute resolution**.

next friend One acting without formal appointment as guardian for the benefit of an infant or person of unsound mind not judicially declared incompetent, or other person under some disability.

no bill This phrase, endorsed by a grand jury on the written indictment submitted to it for its approval, means that the evidence was found insufficient to indict.

"no-fault" proceeding" A civil case in which parties may resolve their dispute without a formal finding of error or fault.

nolle prosequi (also loosely called "nolle pros") Decision by a prosecutor not to go forward with a charge of crime; translates "I do not choose to prosecute."

nolo contendere A plea of no contest. In many jurisdictions, it is an expression that the matter will not be contested, but without an admission of guilt. In other jurisdictions, it is an admission of the charges and is equivalent to a guilty plea.

non compos mentis Not of sound mind.

notice Formal notification to the party that has been sued in a civil case of the fact that the lawsuit has been filed; also, any form of notification of a legal proceeding.

O

objection The process by which one party takes exception to some statement or procedure. An objection is either sustained or overruled by the judge.

"on his own recognizance" Release of a person from custody without the payment of any **bail** or posting of bond.

one-day, one-trial jury service An innovation in many jurisdictions which requires a prospective juror to serve for only one day if he/she is not chosen for a jury, or for only one trial if chosen.

opinion The written decision of an appellate court. The majority or plurality opinion expresses the court's decision. A **concurring opinion** generally agrees with the majority, but usually states different or additional reasons for reaching the same conclusion. A **dissenting opinion** states the opinion of the judges who disagree with the majority. A **per curiam** opinion is an unsigned opinion "of the court."

order A written or oral command from a court directing or forbidding an action.

ordinance A local law adopted by a municipality.

overrule Judge's decision not to allow an objection; also, decision by higher court finding that a lower court decision was in error.

P

pardon A form of **executive clemency**, preventing criminal prosecution or removing or extinguishing a criminal conviction.

parens patriae The doctrine under which the court protects the interests of a juvenile.

parole The supervised conditional release of a prisoner before the expiration of his or her sentence. If the parolee observes the conditions, he or she need not serve the rest of his or her term.

party A person, business, or government agency actively involved in the prosecution or defense of a legal proceeding.

patent A government grant giving an inventor the exclusive right to make or sell his or her invention for a term of years.

peremptory challenge A challenge which may be used to reject a certain number of prospective jurors without giving a reason. Differs from **challenge for cause**.

perjury The criminal offense of making a false statement under oath.

permanent injunction Court order requiring that some action be taken, or that some party refrain from taking action (differs from forms of temporary relief, as a **temporary restraining order** or **preliminary injunction**).

"person in need of supervision" Juvenile found to have committed a status offense rather than a crime that would provide a basis for a finding of delinquency. Typical status offenses are habitual truancy, violating a curfew, or running away from home. These are not crimes, but they might be enough to place a child under supervision. In different states, status offenders might be called "children in need of supervision" or "minors in need of supervision."

petitioner The person filing an action in a court of original jurisdiction; the person who appeals the judgment of a lower court. The opposing party is called the **respondent.**

plaintiff The person who brings a civil lawsuit.

plea In a criminal proceeding it is the defendant's declaration in open court that he or she is guilty or not guilty—the defendant's answer to the charges made in the indictment or information.

plea bargaining The process through which an accused person and a prosecutor negotiate a mutually satisfactory disposition of a case. Usually it is a legal transaction in which a defendant pleads guilty in exchange for some form of leniency. It often involves a guilty plea to lesser charges or a guilty plea to some of the charges if other charges are dropped.

pleadings The written statements of fact and law filed by the parties to a lawsuit.

polling the jury The act, after a jury verdict has been announced, of asking jurors individually whether they agree with the verdict.

"power of attorney" Formal authorization of a person to act in the interests of a person incapable of managing his or her own affairs or property.

precedent A previously decided case which guides the decision of future cases.

preliminary hearing In criminal law, the hearing at which a judge determines whether there is sufficient evidence against a person charged with a crime to warrant holding him or her for trial. The Constitution bans secret accusations, so preliminary hearings are public unless the defendant asks otherwise; the accused must be present, accompanied by legal counsel.

preliminary injunction Court order requiring action or forbidding action until a decision can be made whether to issue a permanent injunction (differs from **temporary restraining order**).

preponderance of the evidence Greater weight of the evidence, the common standard of proof in civil cases.

presentment Declaration or document issued by a grand jury that either makes a neutral report or notes misdeeds by officials charged with specified public duties; ordinarily does not include a formal charge of crime (differs from **indictment**).

pre-trial conference A meeting between the judge and the lawyers involved in a lawsuit to narrow the issues in the suit, agree on what will be presented at the trial, and make a final effort to settle the case without a trial.

prima facie case A case that is sufficient—that is, has the minimum amount of evidence necessary to allow it to continue in the judicial process.

probable cause Sufficient legal reasons for allowing the search and seizure or the arrest of a person.

probate The process of proving that a will is valid and should be carried out. Also, refers more generally to the law governing estates.

probation An alternative to imprisonment allowing a person found guilty of an offense to stay in the community, usually under conditions and under the supervision of a probation officer. A violation of probation can lead to its revocation and to imprisonment.

pro bono publico For the public good. When lawyers represent clients without a fee, they are said to be working pro bono publico.

pro se Person acting as his or her own attorney, whether or not he or she is a lawyer; also, refers to small claims courts in some jurisdictions.

prosecutor A trial lawyer representing the government in a criminal case.

proximate cause The act which caused an event to occur. A person generally is liable only if an injury was proximately caused by his or her action or his or her failure to act when he or she had a duty to act.

public defender Government lawyer who provides free legal defense services to a poor person accused of crime.

Q

quash To vacate or void a summons, subpoena, etc.

R

reasonable man A phrase used to denote a

hypothetical person who exercises qualities of attention, knowledge, intelligence and judgment that society requires of its members for the protection of their own interest and the interests of others. Thus, the test of negligence is based on either a failure to do something that a reasonable person, guided by considerations that ordinarily regulate conduct, would do, or on the doing of something that a reasonable and prudent person would not do.

rebuttal Evidence disproving other evidence previously given or reestablishing the credibility of challenged evidence.

record All of the documents and evidence plus transcripts of oral proceedings in a case.

re-direct examination Opportunity to present rebuttal evidence after one's evidence has been subjected to cross-examination.

referee A person whom the court refers a pending case to take testimony, hear the parties and report back to the court. A referee is an officer with judicial powers and serves as an arm of the court.

rehearing Another hearing of a case by the same court in which the suit was originally heard.

rejoinder Opportunity for the side which opened the case to offer limited response to evidence presented during the **rebuttal** by the opposing side.

remand To send a dispute back to the court where it was originally heard. Usually it is an appellate court that remands a case for proceedings in the trial court consistent with the appellate court's ruling.

remedy Legal or judicial means by which a right or privilege is enforced or the violation of a right or privilege is prevented, redressed or compensated.

remittitur The reduction by a judge of the damages awarded by a jury.

removal The transfer of a state case to federal court for trial; in civil cases, because the parties are from different states; in criminal and some civil cases, because there is a significant possibility that there could not be a fair trial in state court.

replevin An action for the recovery of a possession that has been wrongfully taken.

reply The response of the plaintiff to the defendant's arguments.

respondent The person against whom an appeal is taken.

rest A party is said to "rest" or "rest its case" when it has presented all of the evidence it intends to offer.

return Report to a judge by police on the implementation of an arrest or search warrant; also, a report to a judge in reply to a subpoena, civil or criminal.

reverse Action of a higher court in setting aside or revoking a lower court decision.

reversible error An error sufficiently prejudicial (harmful) to justify reversing the judgment of a lower court.

rules of evidence Standards governing whether evidence in a civil or criminal case is admissible.

robbery Felonious taking of another's property, from his person or immediate presence and against his will, by means of force or fear. (Differs from *larceny*).

S

search warrant A written order issued by a judge that directs a law enforcement officer to search a specific area for a specific piece of evidence.

self-defense Claim that an act otherwise criminal was legally justifiable because it was necessary to protect a person or property from the threat or action of another.

self-incrimination, privilege against The constitutional right of people to refuse to give testimony against themselves that could subject them to criminal prosecution. The right is guaranteed in the Fifth Amendment to the U.S. Constitution. Asserting the right is often referred to as "taking the Fifth."

sentence A court's determination of the punishment to be inflicted on a person convicted of a crime.

sentencing report Document containing background material on a convicted person, prepared to guide the judge in the imposition of a sentence. Sometimes called **pre-sentencing report.**

sequestration Keeping all of the jurors together during a trial to prevent them from being influenced by information received outside the courtroom. Sequestered jurors are usually housed in a hotel, have their meals together, and are given edited copies of newspapers and magazines, all in an attempt to keep them free from outside influences.

sequestration of witnesses Keeping all witnesses (except plaintiff and defendant) out of the courtroom except for their time on the stand, and admonishing them not to discuss their testimony with other witnesses. Also called separation of witnesses. Prevents a witness from being influenced by testimony of a prior witness.

service The delivery of a legal document, such as a complaint, summons or subpoena notifying a person of a lawsuit or other legal action taken against him or her. Service, which constitutes formal legal notice, must be made by an officially authorized person in accordance with the formal requirements of the applicable laws.

settlement An agreement between the parties disposing of a lawsuit.

slander False and defamatory spoken words tending to harm another's reputation, business or means of livelihood.

small claims court A court that handles civil claims for small amounts of money. People often represent themselves rather than hire an attorney.

sovereign immunity The doctrine that the government, state or federal, is immune to lawsuit unless it gives its consent.

specific performance A remedy requiring a person who has breached a contract to perform specifically what he or she has agreed to do. Specific performance is ordered when damages would be inadequate compensation.

standing The legal right to bring a lawsuit. Only a person with something at stake has standing to bring a lawsuit.

stare decisis The doctrine that courts will follow principles of law laid down in previous cases. Similar to **precedent**.

status offenders Youths charged with the status of being beyond the control of their legal guardian—habitually disobedient, truant from school, or having committed other acts which would not be a crime if committed by an adult. They are not delinquents (in that they have committed no crime), but rather are **persons in need of supervision** (pins), **minors in need of supervision** (mins), or **children in need of supervision** (chins), depending on the state they live in. Status offenders are placed under the supervision of the juvenile court.

statute of limitations The time within which a lawsuit must be brought. There are different statutes of limitations for different kinds of lawsuits.

statutory construction Process by which a court seeks to interpret the meaning and scope of legislation.

statutory law Law enacted by the legislative branch of government, as distinguished from **case law** or **common law**.

stay A court order halting a judicial proceeding.

stipulation An agreement by attorneys on both sides of a case about some aspect of a lawsuit, i.e., to extend the time to answer, to adjourn the trial date, to admit certain facts at the trial, etc.

strike Highlighting in the record of a case evidence that has been improperly offered and will not be relied upon.

subpoena A court order compelling a witness to appear and testify.

subpoena duces tecum A court order commanding a witness to bring certain documents or records to court.

summary judgment Order by a judge deciding a case in favor of one side on the basis of the pleadings, before trial and before or after a hearing. A judge issues a summary judgment upon determining there is no factual dispute to be determined by a jury.

summons A notice to a defendant that he or she has been sued and is required to appear in court. A **jury summons** requires the person receiving it to report for possible jury duty.

suppress Forbidding the use of evidence at a trial because it is improper or was improperly obtained (see also **exclusionary rule**).

sustain Court order allowing an objection or motion to prevail.

T

temporary relief Any form of action by a court granting one of the parties an order to protect its interest pending further action by the court.

temporary restraining order A judge's order forbidding certain actions until a full hearing can be held. Usually of short duration. Often referred to as a T.R.O.

testimony Evidence given by a witness under oath; does not include evidence from documents and other physical evidence.

third-party claim An action by the defendant that brings a third party into a lawsuit.

title Legal ownership of property, usually real property or automobiles.

tort An injury or wrong committed on the person or property of another. A tort is an infringement of the rights of an individual, but not founded on a contract. The most common tort action is a suit for damages sustained in an automobile accident.

transcript The official record of all of the testimony and events that occur during a trial or hearing.
trial de novo A new trial.
true bill An **indictment** by a grand jury.

V

vacate To set aside.
verdict Conclusion, as to fact or law, that forms the basis for the court's judgment. A **general verdict** is a jury's finding for or against a plaintiff after determining the facts and weighing them according to the judge's instructions regarding the law.
venire A writ summoning persons to court to act as jurors. More popularly, the term is used to refer to the people summoned for jury duty.
venue The proper geographical area—county, city, or district—in which a court with jurisdiction over the subject matter may hear a case.
voir dire Process of questioning potential jurors so that each side may decide whether to accept or oppose individuals for jury service.

W

waiver Intentionally giving up a right.
waiver of immunity A means authorized by statute by which a witness, before testifying or producing evidence, may relinquish the right to refuse to testify against himself, thereby making it possible for his testimony to be used against him in future proceedings.
warrant Most commonly, a court order authorizing law enforcement officers to make an arrest or conduct a search; an affidavit seeking a warrant must establish probable cause by detailing the facts upon which the request is based.
with prejudice Applied to orders of judgment dismissing a case, meaning that the plaintiff is forever barred from bringing a lawsuit on the same claim or cause.
without prejudice A claim or cause dismissed "without prejudice" may be the subject of a new lawsuit.
witness One who testifies to what he or she has seen, heard or otherwise experienced.
writ A judicial order directing a person to do something.